ADMINISTRATIVE ASSISTANT / SECRETARY CAREER STARTER

by Shirley Tarbell

LEARNINGEXPRESS

LearningExpress • New York

98–65390
CIP

Printed in the United States of America
9 8 7 6 5 4 3 2 1
First Edition

Regarding the Information in this Book
Every effort has been made to ensure accuracy of directory information up until press time. However, phone numbers and/or addresses are subject to change. Please contact the respective organizations for the most recent information.

For Further Information
For information on LearningExpress, other LearningExpress products, or bulk sales, please call or write to us at:
LearningExpress™
900 Broadway
Suite 604
New York, NY 10003
212-995-2566

LearningExpress is an affiliated company of Random House, Inc.

ISBN 1–57685–099–4

7 85555 85099 6

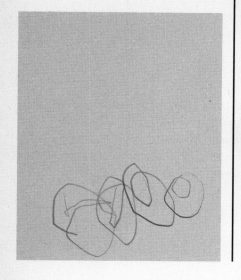

CONTENTS

ABOUT THE AUTHOR | Shirley Tarbell has a Master of Fine Arts Degree from the University of Iowa. Before entering graduate school she was a secretary for years and believes that, without good secretaries, the country would fall apart.

INTRODUCTION

WHY ENTER THE ADMINISTRATIVE ASSISTANT FIELD?

So you're considering a career as an administrative assistant—good for you! This book is designed to help you on your way into this challenging career. You can get into the field as quickly or as slowly as you want. You can go into a six-month to one-year certificate program, a one-year diploma program, or a two-year associate degree program, or you can choose to go on for a four-year bachelor's degree. Whichever you choose, you'll stand an excellent chance of getting a good job when you finish school. You can get good training on the job too. Temporary agencies routinely offer free computer software courses to their employees, and most permanent administrative assistant jobs offer computer training as well. And advanced computer knowledge will make you an employer's dream. This book will give you the knowledge to select the type of training that's right for you.

In chapter one you'll find out just what an administrative assistant is and does. You'll also learn about hiring trends, find sample job descriptions and salaries, and read what some current administrative assistants think about the job.

Chapter two will explain why training is important and how you can decide what kind of training is right for you—and how to succeed in the program of your choice. You'll also see sample training courses and tuition costs from schools across the country.

In chapter three you'll find a list of close to 600 training programs, arranged by state, with contact information.

Chapter four covers state and federal financial aid programs and private scholarships and explains how you can apply for all types of financial aid. Also included are selected addresses, phone numbers, and Internet Web sites to help you in your search for financial aid.

In chapter five you'll find out how to land your first job—the job you really want. The chapter includes sources to search, information on how to write a resume and cover letter, and tips on acing your interviews.

Chapter six offers advice on managing relationships with your boss and coworkers and fitting into the particular culture of your new workplace. You'll learn how to find a mentor and how to promote yourself to get ahead.

In addition, throughout the book, you'll find insights and advice from current administrative assistants. The appendices at the end of the book include helpful resources too: a list of professional associations, accrediting agencies, and state financial aid offices as well as a list of books and periodicals you can refer to for additional information.

So turn the page and begin. This book will give you a good start toward a rewarding and challenging career as an administrative assistant.

CHAPTER | 1

In this chapter, you'll find out what an administrative assistant is and does. You'll also learn about hiring trends; see examples of job descriptions and sample salaries; and discover what current administrative assistants think about the job.

THE NEW FACE OF SECRETARIAL WORK

The administrative assistant field is changing and growing so rapidly in terms of variety and creativity that it's hard to keep up. To even find a definition is difficult these days, so diverse are the jobs under the umbrella title "administrative assistant."

WHAT IS AN ADMINISTRATIVE ASSISTANT?

Let's begin with what an administrative assistant is not. Gone is the stereotypical image of the secretary in the prim suit and starched white blouse, hair in a bun, steno pad eagerly poised to respond to her boss's "Take a letter, Miss Smith." Gone, too, is the image of the dotty Mrs. Wiggins. Remember her from *The Carol Burnett Show* reruns? She was the bimbo-esque secretary of the 1970s who answered the phone (or didn't, as it suited her), did her nails at her desk, and generally drove her boss crazy.

Gone, as I say, are the *images* of these pitiable creatures. They never existed in reality, where the secretary always has been a responsible and important worker. We all know that often the secretary of a company or organization is the dynamo you should go to if you want the real scoop.

According to a 1996 Professional Secretaries International publication, *Benchmarking the Profession: PSI Membership Profile,* the title "secretary" is being replaced in many organizations by the more accurate title "administrative assistant." A recent survey of 847 members of Professional Secretaries International (PSI, the largest organization of professional secretaries in existence) found the following titles being used:

Job Title	Percentage of Use (if known) 1992	Percentage of Use 1997
Secretary		
Executive secretary		
Administrative secretary	55.1%	41.0%
Administrative assistant		
Executive assistant	13.4%	31.6%
Coordinator		
Administrator		
Technician		
Associate	N/A	22.3%
Office manager	N/A	4.8%

Changes in job titles, 1992–1997
Source: Professional Secretaries International press release, 1997

The change in job title reflects recognition by employers that the role of the secretary is changing. The following table indicates the increase in job responsibilities that go along with the new titles:

Responsibilities	Percentage (if known) 1992	Percentage 1997
Creating spreadsheets	72.9%	89.2%
Creating presentation graphics	40.5%	73.1%
Doing desktop publishing	18.9%	30.3%
Composing correspondence		86.9%
Recommending or making purchasing decisions		78.0%
Handling travel arrangements		55.5%
Training others		48.5%
Supervising others		32.9%

Changes in secretarial duties, 1992–1997
Source: Professional Secretaries International press release

The average salary of respondents in the above survey was $28,420. Over half (51.7 percent) earned $26,000 or more, and 26.7 percent earned over $31,000.

The conventional wisdom is that in the future, administrative assistants will have more complex and creative jobs than the old-style secretary, performing some tasks that used to fall to managers and executives—and they probably will earn more than the old-style secretary did. In this chapter, however, we will use the terms "administrative assistant" and "secretary" interchangeably, in order to point out the fact that the distinction between the two is still blurry at best.

WHAT DOES AN ADMINISTRATIVE ASSISTANT DO?

Administrative assistant or secretarial duties have a broad range, and it would be impossible to describe them all; however, following are some general categories.

A *general administrative assistant or secretary* may start out as receptionist or clerk-typist whose tasks are relatively simple; for example, she or he may

- greet clients, customers, or patients and direct them to the correct person or office
- answer the telephone and direct calls to the proper person
- make appointments
- use a personal computer (the typewriter is all but obsolete in secretarial work today) to type correspondence and reports from a Dictaphone or handwritten copy or type forms
- distribute mail

The general administrative assistant or secretary who advances to, or is hired at, a higher level may be responsible, in addition, for

- opening and distributing mail, including personal correspondence
- organizing and maintaining files
- operating fax machines, photocopiers, and telephones with voice mail capabilities
- scheduling appointments
- ordering supplies
- composing as well as transcribing letters (or at least doing heavy editing)
- demonstrating familiarity with a greater variety of computer programs (Word, Powerpoint, Lotus, and Excel are now necessary skills in many offices)
- running spreadsheet software (the electronic version of an accountant's columnar ledger, pencil, and calculator for bookkeeping and budgeting, tracking sales, preparing financial statements, and analyzing financial problems)

- using database management, desktop publishing, and graphics computer programs
- making travel arrangements for the boss or (in a large enough company) being a full-time "travel secretary" for a number of executives (researching timetables and fares for airlines, hotels, and tour and travel agencies, on the computer or by telephone)
- giving information to callers about the company or organization—and knowing when *not* to
- contacting and dealing with clients
- arranging conference calls
- transcribing—and in some cases creating—the department or company newsletter

Following is a sample classified ad you might find on the Internet, describing the job of a general secretary/receptionist in the entertainment field.

Secretary/Receptionist

Industry: Entertainment

Function: Administrative

Responsibilities: Meeting Planning/Event Production

Fast-paced ISO full-time (M–F 9–5) secretary/receptionist. Telephones, word processing (experience required), filing, errands, mail, etc.

Requirements: Individual who is extremely reliable, has excellent communication skills, is outgoing and organized, and has a good appearance and image. Two (2) years office experience required. Start immediately—$20,000 plus benefits.

Interestingly, this job pays only $2,000 a year less than the county legal secretary position described later in this chapter, demands fewer years of training and experience, and sounds a good deal less stressful.

Here's an ad from the *Seattle Times* for a general administrative assistant.

Position: Administrative Assistant, Production Office

A growing food manufacturing facility has immediate opening for an entry-level administrative assistant. Responsibilities include daily data entry of the previous and next day's production and support of managers and supervisors in the packaging/production office. Ideal candidate has excellent organizational and communication skills, and computer proficiency.

Start at $9 an hour, excellent benefits, and free soup.

Maybe the job doesn't *sound* very exciting, but it seems to me a company that offers free soup to its employees is worth checking out! It's probably an entrepreneurial company and thus may offer a chance for advancement, so it would be doubly smart to take a look.

An *executive administrative assistant* or *secretary* may (in addition to many of the tasks of a general administrative assistant or secretary)

- do highly specialized work that requires a knowledge of technical terminology and procedures
- conduct research
- prepare statistical reports
- train and supervise other clerical staff

A subtype of the executive administrative assistant or secretary, the *corporate administrative assistant* or *secretary*, may

- work directly for the president or chief executive officer (CEO) of a corporation and report to the board of directors
- organize corporate meetings and take minutes at those meetings
- deal with stockholders
- keep a record of stocks and bonds activities
- be responsible for certain aspects of corporate records and reports
- do light bookkeeping
- sometimes travel with the boss to meetings in other cities

AREAS OF SPECIALIZATION

There are several areas of specialization for administrative assistants or secretaries. Some of the most common ones are

- legal administrative assistant or secretary
- medical administrative assistant or secretary
- technical administrative assistant or secretary
- temporary administrative assistant or secretary

All these specialties will share some of the tasks of the general administrative assistant or secretary and will have additional important responsibilities.

Legal

A legal administrative assistant or secretary will

* have specialized knowledge of various types of law
* type sensitive, confidential correspondence from lawyer to client
* prepare legal papers such as summonses, complaints, motions, and subpoenas under the supervision of an attorney
* review legal journals and assist in other ways with legal research

In an issue of the *Maine Sunday Telegram*, the following ad appeared, describing a legal administrative assistant or secretary position open in a county courthouse in a small city in Maine.

Regional Court Administrator–Judicial Secretary

This position will provide secretarial support for the justices of the Superior Court.... The position involves transcribing correspondence, maintaining confidential files, receiving, screening, and routing incoming calls and personal callers, distributing mail, and providing other necessary secretarial support to the justices of the Superior Court.

Candidates must be highly conversant with word processing and other PC skills; must have excellent typing (minimum 65 wpm), shorthand, and machine transcription skills. Excellent communication and interpersonal relations skills along with knowledge of legal English, punctuation, spelling, and legal research skills are also necessary. The applicant must have extensive secretarial experience, preferably as an administrative secretary.

Salary begins at $10.88 (salary range $10.88 to $14.90) hourly (about $22,500 to $30,700 per year), plus state fringe benefit package. Value of the state's biweekly contribution for employee benefits is as follows: health insurance $132.92, dental insurance $8.63, and retirement 22.03% of salary....

The following ad was placed on the Internet by an employment agency; the pay's even better (although you should take note of the location, where the cost of living is probably high).

Legal Secretary

Work Location: Downtown Los Angeles

Qualifications: Prefer three to five years prior legal secretarial experience (specifically insurance defense). Will use Microsoft Office/97 (will train). Must know trial work. Will work mainly with Superior Court.

Responsibilities: Legal secretary to the managing partner. Will work on insurance defense (personal injury, auto accident, construction defects). Fifty percent of day working with partner; other half handling overload files of other attorneys.

Compensation: $3,000 per month (flex depending on experience) plus great benefits!

Medical

A medical administrative assistant or secretary will

- have specialized knowledge of medical terminology
- transcribe dictation and prepare correspondence for physicians or dentists
- assist physicians or medical scientists with reports, speeches, articles, and conference proceedings
- record simple medical histories directly from patients
- arrange for patients to be hospitalized
- be familiar with medical supplies
- be familiar with insurance rules, billing practices, and hospital or laboratory procedures

Here is an example from a classified ad on the Internet in October 1997 for a medical secretary in a nationally known cancer treatment center.

Medical Secretary

Provide medical secretarial support for attending physicians in several departments (e.g., Medicine, Surgery, Pediatrics). Responsibilities include screening visitors and phone calls; scheduling patient appointments and admissions; attending patient office sessions; and scheduling special procedures, laboratory tests, and outpatient surgical procedures. Requires a high school diploma and one year medical secretary experience, with solid Dictaphone transcription, word processing (WordPerfect, Word, etc.), and communication skills. Knowledge of medical terminology essential.

Location: New York

[No salary is listed for this job—presumably it would depend on the applicant's experience and qualifications.]

Technical

A technical administrative assistant or secretary may

- assist engineers or scientists by preparing correspondence
- maintain the technical library
- gather and edit materials for scientific papers

The following ad appeared in an October 1997 edition of the *Seattle Times*, describing a job that demands both medical and technical administrative assistant or secretary qualifications.

Administrative Assistant

[A] dynamic eastside [Seattle] medical device company developing unique implantable devices for the treatment of cardiovascular disease is looking for an enthusiastic, energetic individual to join our Clinical Affairs team. Responsibilities include basic administrative duties for the Clinical Research and Clinical Engineering Department, such as correspondence composition and word processing, travel arrangements, transcription of dictation from tapes, answering phones, and filing. This individual will also support field clinical engineers by handling data as it arrives from the field, preparing shipments and transfers of field product, and coordinating communication between field and internal staff. The qualified applicant must have a minimum of five (5) years experience in an administrative support role, excellent written and verbal communication skills, advanced knowledge of word processing and spreadsheets, strong attention to detail, and the ability to work independently and manage several projects simultaneously. Knowledge of medical terminology or experience in a medical or clinical setting is a plus. Database experience is also preferred.

Offers competitive compensation and an outstanding benefits package including medical, dental, and life insurance, 401(k), tuition reimbursement, and equity.

Other Jobs

Additional permanent, full-time, administrative assistant or secretarial job descriptions, recently gleaned from various sources, include:

- From the Internet in October 1997: Administrative assistant to executive vice president/division general manager of an international medical products firm in Ohio; pay rate $30,000 to 35,000 a year.
- From the October 12, 1997, *Honolulu Advertiser*: Administrative assistant in fast-paced office in Honolulu, Hawaii; pay rate $22,000 a year to start—increases possible.

* From the Internet in October 1997: Feature film contact administrative assistant in New York; pay rate $40,000 a year +. The ad says, "Throw away those suits and cleaning bills, and put on those jeans and funky clothes."

A further scanning of the classified ads in the *Seattle Times* and the *Honolulu Advertiser* reveals ads for secretaries/administrative assistants to work in

* an office of the *Seattle Times* itself
* an airline catering service ($40,000 a year)
* a biomedical manufacturer
* the Washington Athletic Club
* a computer software engineering firm
* a new music museum

Temporary

In addition to the types of administrative assistant or secretary positions outlined above, it is possible to be a temporary administrative assistant or secretary working for one or more of the many staffing agencies now in existence. A temporary secretary will perform many or most of the duties outlined above. In the October 1997 issue of *Secretary* magazine, Maureen Decola Harrison relates some advantages of temporary employment:

* It keeps work interesting.
* It offers some schedule flexibility.
* It can be a "bridge" during a transition period.
* It can lead to a permanent job—if you're not sure what career you wish to pursue, temporary jobs can give you a chance to try out several.

A delightful married couple I know, Byron and Valerie Demmer, decided some 15 years ago that they wanted to travel and to live something other than a mainstream life, so they went to work for temporary agencies and love the freedom it gives them. They have lived in California, Colorado, New Mexico, Missouri, Massachusetts, and New York, doing temporary clerical and secretarial work while pursuing their interests in art and philosophy, disciplines that add richness to their lives but don't always pay the bills.

The couple has noticed that in the last few years temporary work is more plentiful than ever, due to the proliferation of temporary agencies. Whereas Kelly

Services, Manpower, and a few others were once their main sources of employment, now there are many more agencies to choose from. They like the variety of work and the ability to pick and choose. "If you don't like the job, it's okay—you know you're not stuck," Valerie says. "On the other hand, if you decide you want to settle down, there are a lot of jobs that are 'temporary to permanent.'" This change has occurred in the last 10 years, Valerie says. "In the old days, the temporary agencies didn't like it if you took a job with an employer they sent you to. Nowadays, employer and employee can try each other out. If there's a good fit, you can make the position permanent with the blessing of the agency that sent you." And Byron points out that temporary agencies now offer benefits, something that was not done in the past.

By doing temporary work, you can pick up a greater variety of skills than in almost any other clerical occupation. As will be discussed in chapter two, many temporary agencies now make computer software and other types of training available to their employees at no charge.

As you can see, there is a great deal of room in the secretarial field for variety and creativity; there is also, as discussed below, room for advancement. You can, with the right training (we'll discuss how to get it in chapter two), be anything from corporate administrative assistant or secretary working directly for the president of a multinational firm with headquarters in, say, Chicago, to administrative assistant or secretary to a film producer in Hollywood or New York, to office manager of a small veterinary clinic in Idaho. As a temporary administrative assistant or secretary, you can wear all these hats and more. Your salary may range anywhere from $16,000 to $40,000 a year or more. In fact, Eleanor Vreeland, former chairperson of the prestigious Katharine Gibbs School and now consultant and editorial advisory board member of that college, says that some executive administrative assistants, for example an administrative assistant or secretary to a chairperson of the board of a large corporation, can make up to $80,000 or $90,000 a year. And you can live anywhere in the U.S. or abroad and be certain of employment.

WHAT PERSONAL ATTRIBUTES MUST AN ADMINISTRATIVE ASSISTANT HAVE?

Deborah Conger, who was once a secretary and is now the elected county recorder of Johnson County, Iowa, says her ideal administrative assistant or secretary would be

- trustworthy and honest, ethical
- someone who will make me look good, who is supportive of my goals

* smart; someone who is not naive and whose opinion I can trust
* dependable
* accurate
* diplomatic and tactful, with good communication skills
* someone with a track record

Other characteristics that might be added:

* a willingness to learn, to take instruction, and to follow directions
* flexibility
* creativity and imagination that stops just short of kookiness, though there are offices in which even kookiness is a plus
* initiative, with an ability to work independently
* a talent for getting along with a variety of people

These latter attributes are all intangibles, of course, but they are even more vital to success in secretarial work than is technical knowledge of equipment or even specific work skills (you can be taught those). And if you have or develop these personal attributes, you'll succeed in virtually any secretarial position, provided the company or organization you work for is at all forward-thinking.

ADVANCEMENT OPPORTUNITIES

In most companies and organizations of moderate or large size, there is chance for advancement from, say, clerk-typist or receptionist to administrative assistant or secretary, or from a lower-level administrative assistant or secretary to a higher-level one. There's a lot of room for advancement within the field if you do two things:

1. *Learn about the business.* Even if you have fairly routine duties, it's wise to learn as much as you can about aspects of the business or organization outside your job description. Learn about management's philosophy, about how clients or customers are acquired, and about how products are produced or services provided. Showing interest in the business or organization as a whole is the surest way to advance and to gain the skills to succeed once you do advance. (If you have no interest in what your employer does, whip out those classified ads! There is no greater hell than a lifetime of working for a company whose product bores you or whose policies you find offensive.)

2. *Upgrade your skills*, not only those needed for your current job but those needed for a better one. Be sure your office-related skills are first-rate, and work toward acquiring proficiency in other areas as well, such as research, writing and speaking effectively, purchasing, bookkeeping, and whatever else is relevant to the business or organization as a whole. Especially important is continuing to upgrade your computer skills—computer literacy is an absolute must these days.

When you feel you're ready to advance—and if you really *want* to (and there's nothing the matter with staying right where you are, if you're happy)—apply for a job with more responsibility and a higher salary, a job working for a higher-level supervisor within your company or organization, or a more challenging job with another firm or organization. In other words, you don't have to wait to be promoted. You can promote yourself!

There is some controversy about the chance for advancement from administrative assistant or secretary to other job titles in a company or organization. It's true that in some companies and organizations, you may be put into the category "secretary" and find your special knowledge and expertise ignored. If possible, steer clear of those places, because whether you remain a secretary or not, the people there won't respect you. There is good potential for advancement in the more enlightened companies and organizations, however.

Jo Ann Beard is now managing editor of the *Social Psychology Quarterly*, a journal of the American Sociological Association, a job she considers at least partly an administrative assistant position. She also was managing editor of a science journal at the University of Iowa a few years ago. She has done secretarial and administrative assistant work for over 20 years and got a master's degree in English and expository writing while continuing to work. She's had good jobs and bad. (In one, her duties included "getting bagels every morning and guarding the boss's car when she parked it illegally!")

Jo Ann's training included some typing and shorthand classes in high school. But she says:

> I have found that most of my training comes on the job. With a basic knowledge of computers (which I learned on the job), I am able to easily step into any job, permanent or temporary, and begin learning office procedures. My secretarial work has been satisfying to me for two reasons: I enjoy organizing details and actually do enjoy doing

paperwork, and secretarial jobs have given me a great deal of free-dom in my off-hours to pursue other interests. I don't have to take my work home with me. I have never had a secretarial job that I could not leave at the office when five o'clock rolled around. That's important for me, because I'm a writer and I need to focus on that when I'm not at my job.

In her last job, Jo Ann traveled several times to assist in conferences her boss was planning and to attend meetings with other administrative assistants and secretaries. "Baltimore, Washington, D.C., and New York are all places I've visited as part of my duties. And I've had other interesting experiences. Several years ago, when I was working as a secretary for a local arts organization in the Midwest, I was able to meet the performers and artists who were brought in for concerts, workshops, lectures, and other events."

As Jo Ann's experience reflects, with the greater demand for complex skills, especially computer skills, administrative assistant work can be challenging and creative. And you'll be able, with enough drive, to move into different kinds of work if you wish. *The Merriam-Webster Secretarial Handbook* asserts that this is the case, especially for talented individuals in fields such as publishing, fashion design, personnel, television, and newspapers. Small entrepreneurial companies also frequently promote from within, because each person, from lowest to highest rank, tends to wear more than one hat. Also, although men are joining the secretarial ranks in ever greater numbers, this has been, for many years, a traditionally female field, and increased recognition of women's talents means more advancement opportunities.

But don't forget: If you're ambitious, there are plenty of creative positions and excellent salaries within the administrative assistant category. It's not uncommon to make $40,000 a year, and as mentioned above, $80,000 to $90,000 is possible if you have the drive. Consider advancing into a more interesting industry or to a job with more perks. Working for the CEO of a large corporation or working on the support staff of one of the "glamour" industries can pay off in other than monetary ways as well. In a recent article in *Cosmopolitan*, Fawn Fitter writes about what's possible for ambitious administrative assistants:

> In addition to hefty paychecks, they may also receive enviable perks: front-row seats at sold-out concerts, the chance to meet celebrities (the secretary to the president of a prestigious music school has

mingled with Bonnie Raitt and Sting), invitations to black-tie fund-raisers, and box seats at sporting events.

Even if you don't go into one of the "glamour" jobs, administrative assistant positions frequently yield perks you might not think of.

HIRING TRENDS—WHAT DO THE EXPERTS SAY?

There is consensus among experts—from the Bureau of Labor Statistics to officials of secretarial schools—that with increasing automation, the nature of administrative assistant/secretarial work is changing and will continue to change. The administrative assistant or secretary is freed from many routine tasks, such as tedious retyping of letters the boss has revised or formatting periodic reports and tables anew each time (computer templates take care of that). The administrative assistant or secretary can spend time on more responsible and creative tasks, such as setting up and conducting meetings with clients or customers, composing letters and reports as well as transcribing them, doing desktop publishing and creating presentation graphics, and setting up databases. And according to the Bureau of Labor Statistics, job openings for administrative assistants/secretaries are on the increase, especially for medical and legal administrative assistants/secretaries. Through the year 2005, job openings overall are expected to increase 12 percent, and for the latter two occupations 68 percent in the medical field and 47 percent in the legal field.

Regarding automation, the Bureau's 1996-1997 report concludes:

> [M]any secretarial job duties are of a personal, interactive nature and, therefore, not easily automated. Duties such as planning conferences, receiving clients, and transmitting staff instructions require tact and communication skills. Because automated equipment cannot substitute for these personal skills, secretaries will continue to play a key role in the office activities of most organizations.

Ray Meyer, director of admissions at the Dallas-based Executive Secretarial School—a well-known and well-respected ACICS-accredited junior college in operation for the last 37 years—points out that with the advent of the computer, the executive administrative assistant or secretary position has expanded to include new duties that are often managerial and says that the technological advances in secretarial work will lead to *more*, not fewer, jobs for secretaries/administrative assistants. Eleanor Vreeland, the above-mentioned consultant to Katharine Gibbs School, asserts that although we have moved from typewriters to the new technology, someone still has to coordinate all the output, whether that person's title be "secretary," "administrative assistant," or something else.

Just look in the classified ads in your town or city newspaper, and you will see that there is always a long list of available jobs for administrative assistants/secretaries. People who predict that these workers will be replaced by the computer are probably the same people who predicted that computers would lead to a "paperless office." We all know there's now a proliferation of paper such as the world has never known. And it all has to be dealt with in some way—organized and coordinated, typed and revised and polished, and filed so that it can be found again. And that job, as Vreeland pointed out, is likely to be given to an administrative assistant or secretary.

HOW CAN YOU BECOME AN ADMINISTRATIVE ASSISTANT?

You might be lucky (or think you're lucky) and get a job right out of high school or even (less likely) without graduating from high school. And it may be a job you like—for awhile. But it's doubtful you'll get far these days unless you obtain some sort of advanced training.

Here are the steps to take for landing a great job:

* Graduate from high school or get a General Educational Development certificate (GED)—that is, a high school equivalency diploma. This step really is a must if you want to have the best chance at promotions and raises. (See the following section, How to Get a General Educational Development Certificate.)

* Check out training programs—the best ways to do this are discussed in chapter two. You'll get much further if you obtain a certificate or diploma (usually a six-month to one-year program) or, better yet, an associate degree (a two-year program) or a bachelor's degree (a four-year program). Take some time deciding which would best suit you—think about what you *really* might like to do eight hours a day and where you'd like to live.

* Apply to training programs—some tips on producing a successful application are discussed in chapter two.

* After training, conduct a job search—some good ways to do this are discussed in chapter five.

* Get the job you want—methods for accomplishing this goal also are discussed in chapter five.

How to Get a General Educational Development Certificate (GED)

In order to earn an equivalency diploma, in most states you must complete a battery of tests in math, reading, grammar (including writing skills), social studies, and science. In addition to knowledge in these subject areas, you may be asked to document instruction in health, civic literacy, and career education. In your community, classes or individualized study will probably be available to assist you in preparing for the GED test. In addition, public television series often offer study materials and educational support through phone contact and occasional teacher/student face-to-face meetings on campus. Technical colleges offer these services and are generally official GED test sites.

In many places, adults who did not graduate from high school but who have learned skills equivalent to those expected of high school graduates may be evaluated and given credit for skills learned on the job, through raising a family, or from their own self-directed learning.

What Kind of Work Environment Should You Choose?

Whatever your situation, whether you're 18 or 61, whether you're in training, preparing for your first job, or looking for a change, you need to give some serious thought to what kind of office environment best suits you. It's important to give this matter more than just surface consideration. For example, it might sound exciting to work in a high-pressure law firm such those depicted on TV or in a "glamorous" film studio. However, if you think hard about it, you might find you're temperamentally more suited to a small, nonprofit organization in which you meet and interact with clients and wear several hats, or even in some kind of outrageous environment like the one described in the 1997 novel *Hoopi Shoopi Donna* in which fictional secretary Sandy Flynn

> …worked in the administration office at the Forest Park Zoo and… once had to help chase a chimpanzee who'd escaped into the adjacent neighborhood and was found… two blocks away in a drugstore's toy aisle, swinging a plastic golf club with such concentration and skill that everyone just stood there and marveled at its ability.

It's fiction, but in real life *somebody* has to be the zoo secretary, and if you like animals….Well, the point is obvious: There's great variety in secretarial work, and it's important to look hard for something that suits you. Too many people settle for less than they're capable of or, conversely, toil joylessly at a job they're told they *should* want—usually fast-paced, high-pressure, "ambitious" work—rather than examining their own interests and dreams.

In our interview, Valerie Demmer described a real-life example of the office from hell, working as a temp for a guy who dictated while jogging, driving, and vacationing, whose motto for himself and for everyone else was "*Never* sit idle. If you're not busy, at least look busy." The tension in that office was as thick as cigar smoke at a 1940s political convention.

In contrast, I once worked as a secretary in a state university statistics department, where it was perfectly okay to read a magazine or even a book at your desk on slow days. I read Stephen King's *The Shining*—all 300-plus scary pages—during my first two weeks. My boss would come out of his office and ask for periodic updates on the plot. There was what most people would think of as a down side to all this, however. When the workload was especially heavy, I was expected to do overtime whenever asked—this entailed, at times, coming in at 4 a.m.! That job suited my temperament, but you might prefer a fast-paced work atmosphere such as that created by Valerie's jogging boss—some people thrive on speed and stress— or at least something a bit more structured.

To focus on the type of internship you want to go into (if you're in school) or the job you're suited for, start by making a list of preferences. The questionnaire near the end of this chapter will help you get started on your list.

Offices vary greatly in their level of formality. Below are some basic types of offices you have to choose from.

The Traditional, Large, Formally Structured Corporation

In the old days, a large corporation—at least a good one—functioned as a family, with the president or CEO as a benign patriarch or (much more rarely) matriarch. Workers could count on the company to offer excellent benefits, job security, and pension plans for a comfortable retirement. Now, in this day of outsourcing and downsizing, such ideal circumstances are rare. Still, a good large corporation can offer advantages that a smaller business simply can't afford—for example:

+ a higher salary
+ better benefits—more days of sick leave and vacation, superior insurance and retirement programs
+ greater opportunity for advancement *if* the hierarchy is not too rigid—at any rate, greater opportunity within your category
+ more departments to transfer to if the one you're in doesn't suit you
+ better equipment, so your job will be easier and you can be more creative

Drawbacks can (but do not necessarily) include:

* a more conservative set of rules
* less variety in the work because of the large, usually specialized work force
* sometimes *less* chance for advancement, if the hierarchy is extremely rigid
* a more impersonal atmosphere
* the need to spend more money on clothing

The Traditional Medium-Size Company

This kind of company can offer many of the same benefits as the large corporation, but it hasn't got money for all of them. Advantages of a medium-size company over a very large one can include:

* somewhat more relaxed rules
* a more personal atmosphere
* a less rigid dress code, so you don't have to spend a fortune trying to look like you just stepped out of the pages of *Vogue* or *GQ*

Drawbacks can but do not necessarily include:

* a lower salary
* fewer benefits
* less chance for advancement
* fewer funds for state-of-the-art equipment

The Traditional Very Small Business

Some small businesses are foundering these days, but if you find one that's successful, the advantages over a larger business can be substantial. These can include:

* greater variety of work, because of the small work force
* more responsibility and an opportunity to learn a wider range of skills
* a more personal atmosphere
* a less rigid dress code

Drawbacks can include:

* a lower salary
* fewer benefits
* less chance for advancement because there simply aren't enough slots
* sometimes (not always) less job stability

The Government or State Institution Office

These offices are quite different from those in any for-profit business, and they can offer all sorts of atmospheres. Generally, government or state office jobs (such as those at public universities) offer the following:

- good pay
- good benefits
- job security (though lately downsizing has been happening here too)
- a fairly relaxed work atmosphere (not always, though—it depends on the bureaucrat in charge)
- a less-than-rigid dress code
- good chances for advancement within your job category and even outside it, because of a formal testing system for various kinds of jobs

Drawbacks can include:

- a tendency toward a more cumbersome bureaucracy
- less efficiency in the workplace, which can be frustrating—usually, again, these offices are nonprofit, so there's not as much incentive to economize with money or time as in a large corporation
- good pay, but no chance for *great* pay

The Nontraditional or Entrepreneurial Office

Jobs in these offices can be fun or a daily nightmare, depending on the style of management and the stability of the business. They can be large or small (many computer companies provide a nontraditional work atmosphere), though most are small, just-starting-out concerns.

Their advantages over traditional offices of any size can include:

- greater opportunity to move up
- greater flexibility of work rules
- greater opportunity for creativity
- a more relaxed atmosphere
- generally a far less rigid dress code

Drawbacks can include:

- lower pay
- fewer (or no) benefits

* less job security (there's that in the world of the large corporation, too, but entrepreneurial companies can go belly-up immediately)

The Temporary Agency Office

It has been said that the temporary work force is the fastest-growing work category in the country, and if you want variety and a certain amount of freedom, a temporary agency might be appealing. The advantages of temporary over permanent work can include:

* the opportunity for a more flexible lifestyle; if you want to take off a few weeks and go hiking in Montana, you can, and it won't harm your work record (if you're like Byron and Valerie Demmer, you can *move* to Montana, if you like)
* a greater variety of kinds of tasks and office atmospheres
* no fear of getting stuck in a job you hate
* the opportunity to shop around for a permanent job you really like
* the opportunity to move from workplace to workplace to find out what kind of office atmosphere is best for you

Drawbacks can include:

* somewhat lower pay, although these days temporary agencies are giving raises
* less (or no) chance for advancement beyond administrative assistant or secretary
* fewer or sometimes no benefits—though this is changing, and many temporary agencies now do have benefits
* (in smaller towns) less job security—in a large city you can be kept busy, but in smaller places there can be terrifying dry spells between jobs

The Home Office

Working at home is ideal for some, especially if you have obligations that make it inconvenient to leave the house for long stretches. Opportunities are out there, though you may have to hustle to find them. Businesses and other concerns are finding out that people who work at home may be more efficient and productive than those who come into the office with all its attendant stresses and woes. (An added perk for employers is that they don't have to pay rent on the space you're sitting in.) Many organizations are now hiring at-home employees for various kinds of secretarial work involving computer operations, even setting the worker up with a home office equipped with a computer hooked into the main office.

If you choose to work at home, there are two ways to go about it: freelance or working for a company or organization.

The advantages of working at home include:

* freedom to set your own hours
* greater variety of work (if you freelance)
* freedom from restrictive rules about breaks, length of lunch hours, taking off for appointments, and so forth (if you freelance)
* freedom from the stress of office politics
* being able to work in your bathrobe with your dog, Bob, at your feet

The drawbacks can include:

* less job security (if you freelance)
* few or no benefits (if you freelance)
* lower pay (especially if you freelance—however, companies who hire home workers frequently pay well and do provide benefits)
* cabin fever from staying home too much

Deciding on a Work Environment

The above is a very general summary of types of office environments; of course the list is not exhaustive (administrative assistants/secretaries are needed in hospitals, churches, and charitable institutions and in such diverse concerns as auto body shops, riding stables, bakeries, massage parlors, and funeral homes), and there are many exceptions and much overlap. And of course the size of a company or institution is not *necessarily* an indication of its level of formality or rigidity of rules. A small law office can be more formal, for example, than an office in a large advertising agency or one in a giant university. And a huge corporation that got its start outside the mainstream—such as Celestial Seasonings or Microsoft—can be extremely informal.

The real point is, there's great variety in office atmospheres and in kinds of administrative assistant/secretarial jobs. And administrative assistants/secretaries are needed all over the nation. With the right training, you won't be limited in the type of office you work in, or where you choose to live. Wherever you go, they'll need you. Answer the questionnaire on the next page to find out what the best work environment is for you.

Personal Preference Questionnaire

Circle the answer that best describes your preference or situation:

1. Which do I prefer?

   A. fast-paced work that leaves me exhausted (though satisfied) at the end of the day

   B. a more relaxed job, with enough work to keep me busy and interested, but some time now and then to chat with coworkers

2. Which best fits my chosen lifestyle?

   A. taking time each morning to groom and dress for success

   B. rolling out of bed, showering, throwing something on, and dashing out the door

3. Which of the following best describes my home situation?

   A. I do not have children or anyone else who depends on me on a daily basis

   B. I have children or someone else dependent on me or likely to need my attention at unpredictable times

4. Which of the following best describes my favorite pastimes?

   A. sports and games in which I interact and compete with others

   B. individual sports or such solitary pastimes as reading, painting, and sewing

5. How important is money to me?

   A. very important, and I'm willing and able to work extra hours to make more

   B. important, but not *that* important; a satisfying job and a good balance of work, play, and family life rank first

6. In what kind of environment do I do my best work?

   A. one that's structured and somewhat pressured

   B. one in which I can work fairly independently, with flexible (but not capricious) regulations

Take note of your answers. The questionnaire is not an absolute measure of what kind of job you should look for—there are many other variables—but in general if you answered "A" to most of the questions, then perhaps you'd do better in a more structured and faster-paced (maybe even high-powered) office. If you answered "B" to most of them, then you might want to look into a medium or small office with flexible rules; or a zany, entrepreneurial one; or maybe even a "permanent" temporary job with benefits.

In addition to the above questionnaire and what it reveals, ask yourself this question: Which of the following subjects interests me the most?

Art	New Age
Science	Sports
Finance	Sociology
Law	Religion
Medicine	Environment

There are many other areas, of course—from motorcycle racing to doll-making—but the point is, if a particular subject appeals to you, why not seek a job related to that subject? Of course, if you find yourself in a job related to a field that's completely foreign to you, you could find yourself head-over-heels in love with it as well.

To sum up, it might be tempting to take the first "good" position that's offered. It might be easy, if you're in school, to let a well-meaning counselor talk you into a particular kind of job because it pays the most or is the most stable. But remember that there is as much variety in secretarial jobs as in other kinds of employment, and you stand a much better chance of succeeding in a position that suits *your* interests, lifestyle, and temperament.

THE INSIDE TRACK

Who:	Jo Ann Beard
What:	Managing editor
Where:	*Social Psychology Quarterly,* a journal of the American Sociology Association, Ithaca, New York
How long:	One year (before that, over 20 years of secretarial experience)

Insider's Advice

You can advance in secretarial work. Anyone who says otherwise doesn't know what they're talking about. I moved from being a secretary on a science journal to being the managing editor when my boss was appointed editor of the journal. He knew my skills and abilities and gave me the opportunity to advance to a job with more responsibility and higher pay. My advice: Remember that your job is, in many ways, as important as your boss's, and your boss probably couldn't do hers or his without you.

Insider's Take on the Future

The jobs I've had as secretary and administrative assistant have been flexible and enabled me to pursue my own writing. Of course I'd like someday to write full time, but in the meantime I'm happy to have an administrative assistant career that uses my skills and stimulates me.

CHAPTER | 2

In this chapter you'll learn why training is important and how to decide what kind of training is right for you, and you'll get hints on how to succeed in the program of your choice. You'll also find sample training courses and tuition costs from schools across the country.

ALL ABOUT TRAINING PROGRAMS

The main reason you should consider getting formal secretarial training is that the face of secretarial work is changing at an unprecedented rate. In the old days, when I began office work, a secretary typed, filed, answered phones, and fetched the boss's coffee, and that was pretty much it. An ancient book called *You Can be an Executive Secretary* lists "must have" skills for the secretary as opening mail, taking and typing dictation, filing, having some knowledge of bookkeeping terms, setting up appointments for your boss, and, of course, making coffee. The book advises, "If [your boss] needs three cups of black coffee at his [sic] desk each morning to help him face the rigors of the day, see that he gets it—at the right temperature and precise intensity of black."

WHY YOU NEED TRAINING

These days, things are altogether different. As noted in chapter one, the title "secretary" is routinely being replaced by the more accurate title "administrative assistant" to reflect the complex nature of the work.

Besides knowing computer programs such as Word, Excel, Lotus, and Windows, the administrative assistant may need to generate spreadsheets, charts, and graphs; do desktop publishing using a variety of graphics and drawing software; prepare graphics for presentation at committee meetings, board meetings, and stockholder meetings; and even create databases. He or she may be called upon to research and write reports; substitute for members of management at important meetings, both in the home office and in faraway cities; deal with clients or customers in much more than a reception capacity; organize public events; interview prospective employees; and train and supervise workers once they're hired.

A 1997 article in the *Detroit News* tells of Christine Gough, who started as a secretary in 1983 with Michigan Sugar in Saginaw and was eventually assigned the duties of factory data coordinator, putting together reports on sugar industry activity—something her previous boss used to do. The same newspaper article cited Jan Gaulin, a secretary at computer services giant Electronic Data Systems Corporation in Troy, Michigan, who now puts together projects and trains employees on top of her regular responsibilities as a secretary.

In 1995 the Administrative Development Institute in Holland, Michigan surveyed 174 secretaries in the United States and Canada and found that about 71 percent of office secretaries head up projects and take on some managerial roles. (These secretaries do not necessarily receive management wages, but that's a topic for chapter six.)

Advantages of Completing a Training Program

In secretarial school you'll learn about the wide variety of job opportunities available to you, and you'll get a broader vision of what's possible. You might find you don't want to work in the traditional corporate world. You might decide the fashion or filmmaking industry, or a university department, or a small veterinary clinic is right for you. The variety of courses available in a good secretarial school will expand your ideas about what a secretarial job can be.

Another advantage of formal training is the availability of placement services through the school you attend, as well as internships (sometimes called "externships") for on-the-job training (discussed below) and courses in how to search for a job.

A third advantage is cited by Jennifer Bergin, a student at Casco Bay College in Portland, Maine. Jennifer is just beginning an externship at Property Management Services, Inc., in Portland and says, "You'll feel more comfortable on the job if you're caught up on the latest technology and have had some experience working." This echoes a statement by Eleanor Vreeland, former chairperson of the prestigious Katharine Gibbs School and now consultant and editorial advisory board member of Katharine Gibbs: "Since people just out of high school are unfamiliar with job searching and with going to a job every day, they need special training in order to know how to dress and behave in an office atmosphere. They need to become familiar with how business communicates."

Types of Training Programs

The main types of training available are

- short-term (3 to 6 months), nondegree courses offered by most schools
- the 6- to 12-month program ending in a certificate or diploma
- the 2-year program ending in an associate of arts or associate of science degree
- the 4-year program ending in a bachelor of arts or bachelor of science degree
- internships (sometimes called externships)
- temporary agency courses
- on-the-job training

Short-Term Courses

At most colleges offering associate of arts or associate of applied science degrees (as well as at four-year colleges offering bachelor of arts or bachelor of science degrees), you may take individual courses you feel you need for the kind of job you want, or brush-up courses if your skills have become rusty. In these short courses, you usually don't earn a certificate or diploma, but the courses are valuable nonetheless. Eleanor Vreeland cites classes in business communications, personal development (dress and behavior in the world of work), and computer training as valuable for teaching technical skills and skills in how to succeed in an office environment. Such classes are also a way of finding out what you'd like to do in the future or testing a longer program before committing yourself.

The 6- to 12-Month Certificate or Diploma Program

In a 6-month or 12-month program, you will obtain a certificate or diploma rather than a degree. The course of study might include intensive training in computer basics, personal development, and business communications but with few or no general education courses. For example, at Casco Bay College you can earn a one-year certificate in office technology. The certificate will qualify you for initial employment as a secretary, and the courses are transferable to a degree secretarial program if you want to go on with your training. Here is the 1997 curriculum for the office technology certificate (a total of 34 credits) at Casco Bay College in Portland, Maine, which is typical of short-term certificate curricula elsewhere:

Semester 1

Elementary Accounting

Introduction to Microcomputer Concepts and Applications

Principles of Written Communication or Writing Laboratory

Mathematics of Business

Beginning Document Processing

Office Systems and Procedures

Semester 2

Advanced Computer Applications in Business

Psychology of Living and Learning

Intermediate Document Processing (or elective course)

Machine Transcription

Word Processing

Career Development

The Associate of Arts and Associate of Applied Science Degrees

The associate of arts degree is a two-year degree program and prepares the student, if she or he wishes, to enter the final two years of a four-year program leading to a bachelor's degree.

Following are brief course descriptions for selected courses in a 70-credit-hour administrative assistant/secretarial associate degree program from Waukesha County Technical College in Pawaukee, a suburb of Milwaukee, Wisconsin. These course descriptions should give you an idea of what to expect if you decide to enter an associate degree program.

Microsoft Office Suite I (3 credits)

This course is designed to develop an understanding of the information processing cycle and workflow, terminology, hardware, and related career opportunities. Emphasis is on utilizing Microsoft Office Suite software and the microcomputer operations as they relate to producing mailable business correspondence using proper formats and procedures. Additional time is spent learning how to build presentations with Power Point software.

Notetaking (3 credits)

Notetaking is the beginner's course. In conjunction with the speedwriting theory portion, students learn speedwriting for the purpose of notetaking and for the development of study skills. Notetaking and study skills teach students how to select the key points from oral and written text as well as how to summarize, record, and organize notes most efficiently.

Information Management (3 credits)

Alphabetic, subject, numeric, and geographical filing systems are covered using ARMA's basic alphabetic indexing rules. All phases of a record's life cycle are studied. Hands-on, manual, and electronic jobs reinforce the fundamental principles and practices of effective records management.

Machine Transcription (3 credits)

Instruction is given on the proper use of transcribing equipment with dictated material from various business and professional areas. Students use computers to produce accurate letters, memoranda, tables, and reports from dictation. Emphasis is placed on listening, proofreading, and language skills including word usage, spelling, and punctuation skills. Students also learn proper dictation techniques.

Administrative Office Procedures (3 credits)

Key administrative office skills will be the focus in this course. Students will refine their document production skills, work with mail processing, and develop telephone etiquette. Practical application will be used to reinforce learned skills.

Desktop Publishing (3 credits)

By using a page composition software package, students gain experience with page layout. Students use PC-compatible computers and PageMaker page composition software to develop project-based assignments (flyers, brochures, newsletters, etc.). Appropriate layout and design techniques are covered.

On the next page is a more ambitious, 105-credit-hour, associate of applied science degree curriculum for the office administration/administrative assisting degree at a well-known and well-respected school in Dallas, Texas, the Executive Secretarial School. This curriculum would prepare you for an executive administrative assistant position in a public or private business or professional office.

Incidentally, at the Dallas Executive Secretarial School you can obtain an associate degree in just 13 months. Students attend classes 30 hours a week rather than the usual 15 to 20 hours at most colleges. It is possible to accelerate through an associate degree program at many schools, if you're willing to put in the hours.

General Education Courses	Credits
American Government or Contemporary American History	5
Composition and Rhetoric 1	5
Introduction to Economics	5
Introduction to Philosophy or Introduction to Psychology	5
Introduction to Public Speaking	5
Precalculus	5
Required subtotal	**30**

Technical Program Courses	
Advanced Computer Applications	3
Advanced Word Processing	3
Business Communications	4
Business Law	4
Business Management	4
Business Math Applications	3
Career Skills	3
College Accounting 1 or 2	4
Computer Literacy	3
Document Processing 1	3
Document Processing 2	3
Document Processing 3	3
Document Processing 4	3
Document Processing 5	3
Integrated Office Applications	3
International Business	3
Introduction to Composition	4
Office Administration and Procedures	4
Personal and Academic Skills for Success	3
Shorthand Applications	3
Shorthand Theory	3
Spreadsheet Applications	3
Word Processing	3
TOTAL	**105**

If you're interested in this option, be sure to ask the school of your choice whether it is available before you make your final decision.

To give you a further idea of the course descriptions for an associate degree, following are a few examples from a typical catalog.

Introduction to the Office (fall/spring; 3 credits)

Emphasizes the fundamentals of word processing, its history, current office practices, organization and structure, workflow, equipment, role of the secretary and management, career opportunities, and basic 10-key instruction.

Professional Secretary Certification I (3 credits)

Emphasis given to the behavioral science in business, principles of business law, and governmental controls on business operations.

Desktop Publishing I (fall/spring; 3 credits)

The fundamentals of layout and design techniques as well as the basic operation of a high-end desktop publishing software program.

Basic Excel (fall/spring; 2 credits)

An introductory course to develop skills in creating, revising, and printing spreadsheets, charts, and graphs.

Office Systems Internship (as needed; 3 credits)

On-the-job training in office systems or business-related areas.

Most schools offer a considerable number of options for specialization within the secretarial and administrative assistant associate degree programs. Some typical options follow. (The list is by no means exhaustive.)

Administrative assistant/secretary

Administrative assistant/secretary bilingual

Executive administrative assistant/secretary

Medical administrative assistant/secretary

Legal administrative assistant/secretary

Personnel assistant

Word processing specialist

Desktop publishing

Administrative assistant/secretary with a subspecialty in another field, for example a background of courses in secondary education, travel and tourism, fashion, film, animal care, insurance, accounting, or virtually any other interest

Sometimes the subspecialty courses are part of the secretarial degree; sometimes they are courses you take on your own at the same or another school. Whether you go for a certificate, diploma, or degree in your secretarial training, you may want to branch out into subjects completely different from your secretarial courses. These can give you a leg up in the job market and make your secretarial career more rewarding and creative. Studying a second language, for example, can lead to jobs in other countries or in international organizations in this country. Studying fashion or film can give you an edge in these exciting fields. Casco Bay College, for instance, offers a seven-course certificate in travel and tourism or fashion merchandising designed for students who have obtained an associate of arts degree. Within its associate degree category, the Dallas Executive Secretarial School offers a bilingual option, in which you will use computer software in both English and Spanish, which will prepare you for a job in an international setting. Many other schools offer such programs or fit electives into the training program itself.

The Bachelor of Arts or Bachelor of Science Degree

It is outside the scope of this book to cover all the possibilities offered by a four-year college degree. You can, if you wish, major in business, which will give you a greater chance for advancement from an administrative assistant position to a higher position in a company or organization, perhaps even to a managerial position. Or you can combine courses in an unrelated field (film, dance, philosophy, biology—the list is endless) with secretarial courses and broaden the number of areas in which you can work. Some subjects in which you may be interested, especially within the liberal arts curricula, simply don't pay very well. Being an administrative assistant can help you manage the rent and give you time to pursue a creative goal outside the world of work. Refer back to the interview with Jo Ann Beard in chapter one for an outstanding example of someone who has found a secretarial career fulfilling while pursuing a creative goal outside her regular employment.

If you feel you don't have the time or money to go for a bachelor's degree, take a look at chapter four, which covers the types of financial aid available to students in all fields.

Internships

The term "internship" (sometimes called an "externship"—they're actually the same thing) refers to on-the-job training at the end of study toward a degree. Students, usually near the end of their associate of arts or associate of applied science degree program, go into a real business office to work. One of the main points you should consider when looking at a school is whether it has a good internship program. Also, although there are many factors to think about when choosing the location of a school, one in or near a large city can offer a greater variety of internships. You may work in a doctor's office, a legal office, or a bank or other type of corporation. Wherever you're assigned, the internship will be invaluable experience, providing you not only with on-the-job training but also with business references for a job before you graduate.

Temporary Agency Courses

Temporary agencies routinely offer courses in office skills to their employees and staff members, and you should call around to the different agencies in your area to see what is available. Both Manpower and Kelly Services, for example, offer free software courses in a wide variety of applications. If you apply for temporary work at Kelly Services, you'll first tell them what kinds of jobs you are interested in. Kelly will then test you to see if you have the necessary skills to be sent out on those jobs. If your skills aren't quite up to par, you can learn and practice them on one of the agency's computers, using an interactive tutorial. When you feel you are ready, you can be tested again. The training on any one application (for example, word processing or spreadsheets) can take place in an hour, or in several hours if you feel you need extra time. All computer training at Kelly Services is free.

Manpower has a program called Putting Quality to Work, which consists of an interactive series of training videos. The videos teach employees about behaviors customers have said they want in a worker. According to Manpower, the program increases workers' understanding of the value of their performance on the job and teaches them to be flexible and take initiative. Manpower also has interactive training on a wide variety of computer applications, and the courses are free.

On-the-Job Training

If, after careful consideration, you decide you just want to start work without special training, and if you are certain of the kind of work you want to do and are fortunate enough to secure a job in that field, on-the-job training may be for you. One advantage, obviously, is expense; you're paid as you train, rather than having to pay. Even so, it is advisable—and will probably be necessary somewhere along the way—to get some kind of formal training, because, as discussed above, the nature of secretarial work is changing all the time and you'll need to keep abreast of changes in technology.

How to Choose the Training Program That's Right for You

Having decided secretarial training is a good idea for you, how do you go about choosing a program? Following are the most important questions you should ask about a prospective school and the type of answers you should receive before considering that school.

What are the qualifications of the faculty?

There should be some faculty members with advanced degrees (M.A., M.B.A., Ph.D., J.D., and so on), and some with experience in the working world. The faculty should be accessible to students for conferences. Student Jennifer Bergin says she chose Casco Bay College in large part because of the college's excellent faculty, who have advanced degrees and a great deal of work experience.

What is the student-teacher ratio?

It's important that the student-teacher ratio not be too high. Education suffers if classrooms are too crowded, or if a teacher has too many students to hope to see everyone who wishes to be seen for a private conference. According to one of the top national accrediting agencies, the Accrediting Council for Independent Colleges and Schools, a reasonable student-teacher ratio for skills training is 30 students to 1 teacher in a lecture setting and 15 students to 1 teacher in a laboratory or clinical instruction setting. At very good schools the ratio is even better than the ACICS recommends. At the prestigious Taylor Business Institution, for example, the ratio is 10 students to one teacher.

Does the school offer extensive computer training and the latest technology?

It's a good idea when you are visiting schools—and you should definitely visit the schools you're seriously considering—to ask to see their lab facilities. The most recent and best computer technology and training should be available to students; the labs should include the technology necessary for

- courses in the latest software; at this writing, Microsoft Office (Word, Excel, Powerpoint and Access), Lotus Notes 1-2-3, Lotus Operator, Windows—and new software is coming along all the time
- a good introductory course in microcomputer concepts and applications
- courses in advanced computer applications for business
- a course in desktop publishing
- courses in data entry, spreadsheets, graphics, and drawing

Part of the accreditation process of a school (discussed on the next page) includes evaluation of its technological facilities, as well as of its library and other instructional resources.

Is the school accredited?

It's important that the school you choose be accredited. Accreditation is a rigorous, complex process and ensures sound educational and ethical business practices at the schools involved. It's a process schools undergo voluntarily. Among other things, to be accredited as a business school, the institution must

* offer a post-secondary (that is, beyond high school), business-related education that leads to a post-secondary credential (such as a certificate, diploma, or degree)
* be licensed by the appropriate state education agency
* offer educational programs that help students develop skills to enhance their careers
* have a sufficient number of graduates to allow the accrediting agency to review the results of the institution's program

Some accrediting agencies are national, some regional. The name of the accrediting agency for the school you're interested in will probably be plainly printed on the school's general catalog, or you can obtain the name of the agency by calling the school. In addition, each accrediting agency will send you, free of charge, a directory of the schools it accredits.

If you would like a directory, or if you have a question about the school you've chosen, you may call the agency that accredits that school, and its personnel will help you find the answer to your question. See Accrediting Agencies in Appendix A for names, addresses, and phone numbers of reputable accrediting agencies for secretarial schools.

An important point to remember is that if the school you choose is not accredited, you cannot get financial aid through any of the government programs.

What is the school's job placement rate for graduates?

A school's job placement rate for graduates is extremely important, and when considering a school, whether public or private, you should ask for this information. Usually schools offer placement services free of charge, often for the working lifetime of their graduates. All accredited private schools must place a certain percentage of their students in order to maintain accreditation. There is no set percentage, but it must be what the accrediting agency terms reasonable. It is not unusual for a good school to boast above 90 percent placement of its graduates.

A good job placement office will offer

- resume writing and cover-letter writing assistance
- job leads—full time, part time, permanent, and temporary
- networking opportunities with employers in the area (often begun as a part of an internship while the student is still in school)
- seminars on job-hunting
- career counseling and simulated interviews
- lifetime placement assistance for graduates

Does the school have a good internship program?

The matter of internships is discussed above, but it is worth reiterating that this is one of the main points you should consider when choosing a secretarial training program. The variety of internships makes schools located near a large city especially attractive. As part of the accreditation process, schools must monitor the internship programs to ensure the student is introduced to meaningful work, not simply relegated to filing or other menial tasks. As mentioned above, a good internship will give you an advantage when you go out to look for a job.

Program Costs

Tuition varies according to many factors but especially according to length of the program and the area in which the school is located. Some examples of tuition amounts in various parts of the country were culled from the Internet and from 1997–1998 print college catalogs and appear in the table on the next page. Books, admission fees, lab fees, and such are *not* included in this table. Also, remember that tuition tends to go up every year. Take a look at the following school tuitions among different programs to get an idea of tuition costs for secretarial programs. The "A" in the Award column stands for an associate degree and the "C/D" stands for certificate or diploma. The amount of tuition listed is for the total training program, not a yearly cost.

Only you can decide whether you can afford to go into a training program, but before making a final decision, take a look at chapter four on financial aid. You may be able to afford a better program than you think.

Admission Requirements

Basic admission requirements are quite similar for all good schools. To get an idea of the requirements you will have to meet for your training, take a look at the

Sample Program Costs

Name & Location Of School	Program	Length Of Program	Award	Tuition (1997)
Institute of Career Education, West Palm Beach, FLORIDA	Administrative Assistant	65 weeks	A	$ 9,700
	Legal Secretary	52 weeks	C/D	$7,600
	Medical Secretary	52 weeks	C/D	$8,600
	Medical Transcriptionist	65 weeks	C/D	$10,700
	Med-Legal Office Specialist	26 weeks	C/D	$4,200
	Word Processing Specialist	52 weeks	C/D	$7,600
Executive Secretarial Schools, Dallas, TEXAS	Administrative Assistant	58 weeks	A	$13,125
	Administrative Assistant, Bilingual	58 weeks	A	$13,125
	Administrative Assistant, Legal	58 weeks	A	$13,125
	Administrative Assistant	48 weeks	D	$ 9,375
Casco Bay College, Portland, MAINE	Administrative Assistant	4 semesters	A	$11,900
	Office Technology	2 semesters	C	$5,950
Technical Trades Institute, Grand Junction, COLORADO	Medical Secretary/Receptionist	48 weeks	C/D	$8,465
	Receptionist/Secretary	45 weeks	C/D	$8,260
	Executive Secretary	60 weeks	A	$11.045
	Administrative Assistant	60 weeks	A	$10,990
	Legal Secretary	45 weeks	C/D	$8,285
All California Community Colleges (Private schools NOT included)	Administrative Assistant programs	(Varies according to school)	A & C/D	Fees only (no tuition for residents) $13/unit (Non-resident tuition varies)
MTI Business College of Stockton, Inc., Stockton, CALIFORNIA	Executive Secretary	36 weeks	C/D	$4,703
	Medical Secretary	37 weeks	C/D	$4,954
	Legal Secretary	36 weeks	C/D	$4,953

following, from the Katharine Gibbs School, a school that's been around for over 85 years, has seven locations in the northeastern United States, and is very strong in secretarial training.

In order to be accepted at Katharine Gibbs, you must

- have a high school diploma or its equivalent
- have one of the following (depending on the program to which you are applying):
  1. an acceptable score on the SAT (850 or higher), ACT (17 or higher), CPAt (140 or higher—the CPAt test is administered at the Katharine Gibbs School), or TOEFL (500 or higher) *or*

2. an associate degree with a GPA of 3.0 or higher *or*

3. a bachelor's degree (candidates with bachelor's degrees or higher are exempt from admissions test requirements)

The applicant must then

- complete a formal application and submit it to the admissions office, along with a nonrefundable (except in New Jersey) application fee
- interview with an admissions representative, a process that takes approximately one hour
- be recommended to the school president by the admissions representative
- complete an enrollment agreement
- request and submit an official high school transcript
- provide proof of required immunizations for certain schools

After you've completed the above process, your application will be evaluated by the school president. Acceptances before high school graduation depend upon notification of satisfactory completion of high school requirements. Applicants who have concluded their junior year of high school may apply for early acceptance.

As is the case with all schools accredited by a reputable accrediting agency, after graduation you can make use of Katherine Gibbs's placement service for moving from college to work.

HOW TO MAKE THE MOST OF YOUR TRAINING

Once you are accepted into a program, no matter how long or short, good study habits—habits you may not have cultivated in high school—are a must. Following are some tips.

- Start studying early in the semester. Begin taking notes the first day of class, even if you believe you know the introductory material.
- Establish a special place to study, preferably one in which you do nothing else. It should, of course, be a place in which you won't be distracted. Set a time to study for each class.
- The conventional wisdom says that for each hour you spend in class, you must study two hours outside of class, but some classes will require more.
- Go over your class notes after each class to be sure you understand them. Be sure to do all reading, even if a written assignment isn't involved.

- Schedule breaks, preferably 10 minutes out of every hour. It's best to avoid sessions that are too long—try to schedule several short sessions during the day.
- Study the hardest subject first, rather than putting it off until you're tired.

Learn to take good notes

- You can't write down everything, so just include the important points. Don't try to write in complete sentences—devise your own system of abbreviations.
- As soon as possible after class, edit your notes to make them more clear and complete. Recopying everything you write down may be a waste of time, but reviewing and editing soon after class is not.
- Label notes as to subject matter in the margins to the left, so you'll be able to study more efficiently for tests.
- Look at your syllabus daily and do the reading assignments faithfully. Read ahead if at all possible. Prepare for each class as if there will be a quiz at the end of it.
- Attend lectures regularly. Missing one can cause you to miss others out of simple inertia.
- If you use a standard, 8 1/2 x 11-inch looseleaf notebook, you can rearrange your notes when you're studying.
- Keep notes for each class in a separate notebook, but do not try to carry all the notebooks with you. Besides straining your back, you could lose them all, which would be a disaster!
- Write on only one side of the paper. This way you won't miss anything when you're studying later.

Study with other students

Studying with a group or partner can help you get better grades. (Just be sure your study period doesn't degenerate into a party!) Following are suggestions on studying with other people.

- Set aside a time to meet each week, and be sure to arrive on time.
- Exchange photocopies of notes taken in class, and then review the notes during your study sessions.
- Prepare for tests together—quiz each other with questions that might be on the test.

* Meet in a quiet place and do nothing there except study.

Make use of study resources on campus

* Check on the location of labs and the availability of tutors, videos, and computer programs. Sign up for an orientation session to the campus library and for the computer facilities—this is a must!
* Get to know your professors and advisors. Take advantage of their office hours and ask them lots of questions.

Be kind to yourself

Above all, cultivate good health habits. Eat right and get enough sleep. Schedule time for recreation (not usually a problem, but some students are so driven they forget to have fun). And remember that cramming for tests in all-night study sessions—fueled only by black coffee and caffeine pills—is counterproductive.

THE INSIDE TRACK

Who:	Jennifer Bergin
What:	Associate degree candidate
Where:	Casco Bay College, Portland, Maine
How long:	One and a half years

Insider's Advice

When you're looking for a school, I think picking one in a big town is a good idea, because the externships will be better. Businesses in Portland call Casco Bay College asking for externs, and I'm looking forward to my externship as a secretarial assistant at Property Management in Portland in the spring. I'll work 45 hours during the semester for college credit, and it'll give me excellent experience. The other main qualities to look for in a school are the teachers' qualifications and the equipment you'll be using. The equipment should be state-of-the-art. Visit all the schools you're considering—that's important.

Insider's Take on the Future

I've always wanted to be a secretary. I like the work, and I'm happy I chose it. I'll be getting my associate degree soon, and then I'd like to go on for a bachelor's. I've been lucky to get a scholarship through school that's paid for my training. Prospective students should always look into scholarships before they decide they can't afford to go to school.

CHAPTER 3

DIRECTORY OF ADMINISTRATIVE ASSISTANT/ SECRETARIAL TRAINING PROGRAMS

Now that you've decided to get into a training program, you need to know which schools are available near you. The list that follows mainly contains proprietary (that is, private) schools. To find lists of community colleges, refer to Appendix A under *Financial Aid from State Higher Education Agencies.* You may call any of those offices for directories of schools within your particular state. You can obtain information, as well, on particular schools from helpful books, such as *Peterson's Guide to Two-Year Colleges 1998* and *Peterson's Guide to Four-Year Colleges 1998*, available at most large bookstores and libraries. While the specific schools included in this chapter are not endorsed or recommended by Learning-Express, they are intended to help you begin your search for an appropriate school by offering a representative listing of accredited schools in each state. Since there are so many schools that offer these programs, not all of the schools in the country could be listed here due to space limitations. However, this representative listing should get you started.

ALABAMA

Gadsden Business College
P.O. Box 1575
630 S. Wilmer
Anniston 36202-1575
205-237-7517

Bessemer State Technical College
Dept. of Admissions
Bessemer 35021-0308
800-235-5368

Virginia College
1900 28th Ave. South
Birmingham 35209
205-802-1200

Reid State Technical College
P.O. Box 588
Evergreen 36401-0588
334-578-1313

Gadsden Business College
P.O. Box 1544
750 Forrest Ave.
Gadsden 35901
205-546-2863

Herzing College of Business &
Technology
280 West Valley Ave.
Homewood 35209
205-916-2800

J. F. Drake State Technical College
3421 Meridian St. N.
Huntsville 35811-1584
205-539-8161

Virginia College
2800-A Bob Wallace Ave.
Huntsville 35805
205-533-7387

Education America—Southeast College
of Technology
828 Downtowner Loop West
Mobile 36609-5404
205-343-8200

Draughons Junior College
122 Commerce St.
Montgomery 36104
334-263-1013

Prince Institute of Professional Studies
7735 Atlanta Hwy.
Montgomery 36117-4231
334-271-1670

ALASKA

Charter College
2221 East Northern Lights Blvd.
Suite 120
Anchorage 99508
907-277-1000

University of Alaska Southeast
Ketchikan Campus
Ketchikan 99901-5798
907-225-6177

University of Alaska Anchorage
Matanuska-Susitna College
Palmer 99645-2889
907-745-9726

Univ. of Alaska Anchorage
Kenai Pennisula College
Soldotna 99669-9798
907-262-0311

ARIZONA

Central Arizona College
Dept. of Student Records/Registrar
Coolidge 8528-9779
520-426-4260

Cochise College
Dept. of Admissions
Douglas 85607-9724
520-364-0336; 800-966-7946

Lamson Junior College
1980 W. Main, Suite 250
Mesa 85201
602-898-7000

Academy of Business College
2525 West Beryl Ave.
Phoenix 85021
602-942-4141

American Institute
3443 North Central Ave., Suite 1800
Phoenix 85012
602-252-4986

The Bryman School
4343 North 16th St.
Phoenix 85016-5338
602-274-4300

Cochise College
Dept. of Admissions
Sierra Vista 85635-2317
520-515-5412; 800-966-7943

Chaparral College
4585 E. Speedway Blvd., Suite 204
Tucson 85712
520-327-6866

Interstate Career College
6367 East Tanque Verde Rd., Suite 100
Tucson 85715
520-327-6851

Parks College
6992 East Broadway
Tucson 85710
520-886-7979

Tucson College
7302-10 E. 22nd St.
Tucson 85710
520-296-3261

ARKANSAS

Southern Arkansas University Tech
Dept. of Student Affairs
Camden 71701
501-574-4504

Ozarka Technical College
Dept. of Admissions
Melbourne 72556
501-368-7371

Petit Jean Technical College
P.O. Box 586
Morrilton 72110
501-354-2465; 800-264-1094

Pulaski Technical College
3000 W. Scenic Dr.
North Little Rock 72118
501-771-1000

Shorter College
604 Locust St.
North Little Rock 72114-4885
501-374-6305

CALIFORNIA

Computer Learning Center
222 South Harbor Blvd.
Anaheim 92805
714-956-8060

ConCorde Career Institute
1717 South Brookhurst St.
Anaheim 92804-6461
714-635-3450

Orange County Business College
2035 East Ball Rd.
Anaheim 92806
714-772-6941

Santa Barbara Business College
211 South Real Rd.
Bakersfield 93301
805-835-1100

Southern California College of
Business & Law
595 West Lambert Rd.
Brea 92621
714-256-8830

MTI Collegelton Branch Campus
760 Via Lata #300
Colton 92324-3916
909-424-0123

National Career Education
6060 Sunrise Vista Dr., Suite 3000
Citrus Heights 95610-7053
916-969-4900

Eldorado College
385 North Escondido Blvd.
Escondido 92025
619-743-2100

Santa Barbara Business College
4333 Hansen Ave.
Fremont 94536
510-793-4342

Silicon Valley College
41350 Christy St.
Fremont 94538
510-623-9966

Sierra Valley Business College
Building D, 4747 North 1st St.
Fresno 93726
209-222-0947

Comprehensive Training System
497 11th St., Suite 4
Imperial Beach 91932
619-424-6650

Educorp Career College
230 E. 3rd St.
Long Beach 90802-3140
213-437-0501

Travel and Trade Career Institute
3635 Atlantic Ave.
Long Beach 90807-3417
310-426-8841

Los Angeles ORT Technical Institute
635 South Harvard Blvd.
Los Angeles 90005-2586
213-966-5444

Nova Institute of Health Technology
3000 South Robertson Blvd.
Los Angeles 90034-9158
310-840-5777

Valley Commercial College
1207 I St.
Modesto 95354
209-578-0616

American College of Hotel &
Restaurant Management
11336 Camarillo St.
North Hollywood 91602
818-505-9800

ConCorde Career Institute
4150 Lankershim Blvd.
North Hollywood 91602-2896
818-766-8151

Eldorado College
2204 El Camino Real, Suite 104
Oceanside 92054
619-433-3660

Nova Institute of Health Technology
520 North Euclid Ave.
Ontario 91762-3591
909-984-5027

MTI College
2011 West Chapman Ave., Suite 100
Orange 92668-2632
714-385-1132

Mt. Sierra College
350 North Halstead St.
Pasadena 91107
818-351-9995

Watterson College
150 South Los Robles Ave., Suite 100
Pasadena 91101
818-449-3990

Westech College
500 West Mission Blvd.
Pomona 91766-1532
909-622-6486

California Paramedical and Technical
4550 La Sierra Ave.
Riverside 92505-2907
909-687-9006

Bryman College
3505 North Hart Ave.
Rosemead 91770-2096
818-573-5470

High-Tech Institute
1111 Howe Ave., Suite 250
Sacramento 95825
916-929-9700

MTI Western Business College
5221 Madison Ave.
Sacramento 95841
916-339-1500

Sawyer College
8475 Jackson Rd.
Sacramento 95826
916-383-1909

Western Career College
8909 Folsom Blvd.
Sacramento 95826-9823
916-361-1660

ConCorde Career Institute
570 West 4th St.
San Bernardino 92401
909-884-8891

Skadron College
825 East Hospitality Ln.
San Bernardino 92408
909-885-3896

ConCorde Career Institute
123 Camino De La Reina
San Diego 92108-3002
619-688-0800

Eldorado College
2255 Camino Del Rio, Suite 200
San Diego 92108-3605
619-294-9256

Maric College of Medical Careers
3666 Kearny Villa Rd.
San Diego 92123-1995
619-279-4500

Platt College
6250 El Cajon Blvd.
San Diego 92115-3919
619-265-0107

Bryman College
1245 South Winchester
San Jose 95128
408-246-0859

Western Career College
170 Bayfair Mall
San Leandro 94578-9930
510-278-3888

Santa Barbara Business College
5266 Hollister Ave.
Santa Barbara 93111
805-967-9677

Institute for Business and Technology
2550 Scott Blvd.
Santa Clara 95050-2551
408-727-1060

Coastal Valley College
731 South Lincoln St.
Santa Maria 93454
805-925-1478

Santa Barbara Business College
303 East Plaza Dr.
Santa Maria 93454
805-922-8256

Empire College
3033 Cleveland Ave., Suite 102
Santa Rosa 95403
707-546-4000

Los Angeles ORT Technical Institute
Valley Branch
15130 Ventura Blvd., #250
Sherman Oaks 91403-3301
818-788-7222

MTI Business College of Stockton
6006 North El Dorado St.
Stockton 95207-4349
209-957-3030

Maric College of Medical Careers
2030 University Ave.
Vista 92083
619-747-1555

Maric College of Medical Careers
Vista Campus Branch
1593-C East Vista Way
Vista 92084-3577
619-758-8640

Eldorado College
1901 Pacific Ave.
West Covina 91790
818-960-5173

Nova Institute of Health Technology
12449 Putnam St.
Whittier 90602
310-945-9191

COLORADO
Parks College
Six Abilene St.
Aurora 80011
303-367-2757

Blair College
828 Wooten Rd.
Colorado Springs 80915
719-574-1082

City College of Colorado Springs
6050 Erin Park Dr., Suite 250
Colorado Springs 80918
719-532-1234

Denver Paralegal Institute
105 East Vermijo Ave., Suite 415
Colorado Springs 80903-2012
719-444-0190

Denver Business College
7350 North Broadway
Denver 80221
303-426-1000

Heritage College of Health Careers
12 Lakeside Ln.
Denver 80212-7413
303-477-7240

Parks College
9065 Grant St.
Denver 80229
303-457-2757

Institute of Business & Medical Careers
1609 Oakridge Dr., Suite 102
Fort Collins 80525
970-223-2669

Technical Trades Institute
772 Horizon Dr.
Grand Junction 81506
970-245-8101

CONNECTICUT
Branford Hall Career Institute
One Summit Place
Branford 06405
203-488-2525

Butler Business School
2710 North Ave.
Bridgeport 06604
203-333-3601

Connecticut Business Institute
809 Main St.
East Hartford 06108
203-291-2880

Data Institute
745 Burnside Ave.
East Hartford 06108
860-528-4111

Sawyer School
1125 Dixwell Ave.
Hamden 06514
203-239-6200

Morse School of Business
275 Asylum St.
Hartford 06103
203-522-2261

New England Technical Institute
of Connecticut
200 John Downey Dr.
New Britain 06051-2904
203-225-8641

Ridley-Lowell Business & Technical
Institute
470 Bank St.
New London 06320
203-443-7441

Connecticut Business Institute
447 Washington Ave.
North Haven 06473
203-239-7660

Gibbs College
142 East Ave.
Norwalk 06851
203-838-4173

Huntington Institute
193 Broadway
Norwich 06360
860-886-0507

Connecticut Business Institute
605 Broad St.
Stratford 06497
203-377-1775

Data Institute
101 Pierpoint Rd.
Waterbury 06705
203-756-5500

Porter and Chester Institute
320 Sylvan Lake Rd.
Watertown 06779-1400
203-274-9294

Fox Institute of Business
99 South St.
West Hartford 06110
860-947-2299

Branford Hall Career Institute
995 Day Hill Rd.
Windsor 06095
860-683-4900

DELAWARE
Dawn Training Institute
2400 West 4th St.
Wilmington 19805
302-575-1322

Star Technical Institute
Grayston Plaza
631 W. Newport Pike
Wilmington 19804
302-999-7827

FLORIDA
ATI Career Training Center
2880 Northwest 62nd St.
Fort Lauderdale 33309-9731
305-973-4760

City College
1401 West Cypress Creek Rd.
Fort Lauderdale 33309
954-492-5353

International College
8695 College Parkway, Suite 120
Fort Meyers 33919
941-482-0019

Southwest Florida College of Business
1685 Medical Ln., Suite 200
Fort Myers 33907
941-939-4766

Webster College
2192 North U.S. Rte. 1
North Bridge Plaza
Fort Pierce 34946
407-464-7474

Webster College
2127 Grand Blvd.
Holiday 34691
813-942-0069

Prospect Hall School of Business
2620 Hollywood Blvd.
Hollywood 33020
954-923-8100

ConCorde Career Institute
7960 Arlington Expwy.
Jacksonville 32211-7429
904-725-0525

Flagler Career Institute
3225 University Blvd. S.
Jacksonville 32216-2736
904-721-1622

Jones College
5353 Arlington Expwy.
Jacksonville 32211-5588
904-743-1122

Florida Metropolitan University
995 E. Memorial Blvd., Suite 110
Lakeland 33801
941-686-1444

ConCorde Career Institute
4000 North State Rd. 7
Lauderdale Lakes 33319
305-731-8880

Florida Metropolitan University
2401 North Harbor City Blvd.
Melbourne 32935
407-253-2929

Herzing Institute
1270 North Wickham Rd., Suite 26
Melbourne 32904
407-255-9232

ConCorde Career Institute
285 Northwest 199th St.
Miami 33169-2920
305-652-0055

Florida Computer & Business School
8300 Flagler St., Suite 200
Miami 33144
305-553-6065

Miami Institute of Technology
1001 Southwest 1st St.
Miami 33130-1008
305-324-6781

Southern Technical Center
19151 South Dixie Hwy.
Miami 33157
305-254-0995

International College
2654 E. Tamiami Trail
Naples 33962-5790
941-774-4700

Webster College
1530 Southwest 3rd Ave.
Ocala 32671
904-629-1941

Career Training Institute
3326 Edgewater Dr.
Orlando 32804-6984
407-843-3984

Herzing Institute
1300 North Semoran Blvd.
Orlando 32087
407-380-6315

Southern College
5600 Lake Underhill Rd.
Orlando 32807
407-273-1000

Jones College
5975 Sunset Dr., Suite 100
South Miami 33143
305-669-9606

ConCorde Career Institute
4202 West Spruce St.
Tampa 33607-4127
813-874-0094

Florida Metropolitan University
Tampa College, Brandon
3924 Coconut Palm Dr.
Tampa 33619
813-621-0041

Cooper Career Institute
2247 Palm Beach Lakes Blvd., Suite 110
West Palm Beach 33409
407-640-6999

Institute of Career Education
1750 45th St.
West Palm Beach 33407-2192
407-881-0220

GEORGIA
Herzing College of Business &
Technology
3355 Lenox Rd., Suite 100
Atlanta 30326
404-816-4533

National Center for Paralegal Training
3414 Peachtree Rd. N., Suite 528
Atlanta 30326
404-266-1060

Kerr Business College
2528 Center West Pkwy., Bldg. A
Augusta 30909
706-738-5046

Meadows College of Business
1170 Brown Ave.
Columbus 31906
706-327-7668

Gwinnett College
4230 Hwy. 29, Suite 11
Lilburn 30247
770-381-7200

HAWAII
Denver Business College
419 South St., Suite 174
Honolulu 96813
808-942-1000

Hawaii Business College
33 South King St., 4th Floor
Honolulu 96813-4316
808-524-4014

IDAHO
ITT Technical Institute
12302 West Explorer Dr.
Boise 83713
208-322-8844

Mountain Home Institute of Learning
352 North 2nd E.
P.O. Box 1258
Mountain Home 83647
208-587-7028

ILLINOIS
Chicago College of Commerce
11 East Adams St.
Chicago 60603
312-236-3312

College of Office Technology
1514-20 West Division St., 2nd Fl.
Chicago 60622
312-278-0042

Northwestern Business College
4829 North Lipps
Chicago 60630-2298
773-777-4220

SER Business & Technical Institute
3800 West 26th St., 2nd Fl.
Chicago 60623
312-379-1152

Taylor Business Institute
36 South State St., 8th Fl.
Chicago 60603
312-236-6400

Tyler School of Secretarial Sciences
8030 South Kedzie Ave.
Chicago 60652
312-436-5050

Sanford-Brown College
3237 W. Chain of Rocks Rd.
Granite City 62040
618-931-0300

Northwestern Business College–South
8020 W. 87th St.
Hickory Hills 60457
708-430-0990

Heartland School of Business
211 West State St., Suite 204
Jacksonville 62650
217-243-9001

Commonwealth Business College
1527 47th Ave.
Moline 61265
309-762-2100

Fox Secretarial College
4201 W. 93rd St.
Oak Lawn 60453
708-636-7700

Gem City College
700 State St.
Quincy 62301
217-222-0391

Rockford Business College
730 North Church St.
Rockford 61103
815-965-8616

Sparks College
131 South Morgan St.
Shelbyville 62565
217-774-5112

INDIANA
Indiana Business College
140 East 53rd St.
Anderson 46013
317-644-7414

Indiana Business College
2222 Poshard Dr.
Columbus 47203
812-379-9000

Indiana Business College
4601 Theater Dr.
Evansville 47715
812-476-6000

International Business College
3811 Illinois Rd.
Fort Wayne 46804
219-432-8702

ITT Technical Institute
4919 Coldwater Rd.
Fort Wayne 46825-5532
219-484-4107

Michiana College
4807 Illinois Rd.
Fort Wayne 46804
219-436-2738

Sawyer College
6040 Hohman Ave.
Hammond 46320
219-931-0436

College of Court Reporting
111 W. 10th St.
Hobart 46342
219-942-1459

Indiana Business College
802 North Meridan
Indianapolis 46204
317-264-5656

International Business College
7205 Shadeland Station
Indianapolis 46256
317-841-6400

Professional Careers Institute
2611 Waterfront Pkwy., East Dr.
Indianapolis 46214-2028
317-299-6001

Indiana Business College
Two Executive Dr.
Lafayette 47905
317-447-9550

Commonwealth Business College
8995 North State Rte. 39
LaPorte 46350
219-362-3338

Indiana Business College
830 North Miller Ave.
Marion 46952
317-662-7497

Commonwealth Business College
4200 West 81st Ave.
Merrillville 46410
219-769-3321

Sawyer College
3803 East Lincoln Hwy.
Merrillville 46410
219-947-4555

Indiana Business College
1809 North Walnut St.
Muncie 47303
317-288-8681

Michiana College
1030 East Jefferson Blvd.
South Bend 46617
219-237-0774

Indiana Business College
3175 South 3rd Pl.
Terre Haute 47802
812-232-4458

Indiana Business College
1431 Willow St.
Vincennes 47591
812-882-2550

IOWA
American Institute of Commerce
2302 West First St.
Cedar Falls 50613
319-277-0220

Hamilton College
1924 D St. Southwest
Cedar Rapids 52404
319-363-0481

American Institute of Commerce
1801 East Kimberly Rd.
Davenport 52807
319-355-3500

Hamilton College
2300 Euclid Ave.
Des Moines 50310
515-279-0253

Hamilton College
100 First St. Northwest
Mason City 50401
515-423-2530

KANSAS
Center for Training in Business & Industry
3300 Clinton Parkway Court
Lawrence 66047
913-841-9640

Wright Business School
9500 Marshall Dr.
Lenexa 66215
913-492-2888

Education America–Topeka Technical College
1620 Northwest Gage Blvd.
Topeka 66618-2843
913-232-5858

Remington College
6130 East Central, Suite 202
Wichita 67208
316-681-6700

KENTUCKY
Draghons Junior College
2424 Airway Dr. and Lovers Ln.
Bowling Green 42103
502-843-6750

Southwestern College of Business
2929 South Dixie Hwy.
Crestview Hills 41017
606-341-6633

Kentucky College of Business
115 East Lexington Ave.
Danville 40422
606-236-6991

Kentucky College of Business
7627 Ewing Blvd.
Florence 41042
606-525-6510

Southern Ohio College
309 Buttermilk Pike
Fort Mitchell 41017
606-341-5627

Fugazzi College
406 Lafayette Ave.
Lexington 40502
606-266-0401

Kentucky College of Business
628 East Main St.
Lexington 40508
606-253-0621

Kentucky College of Business
3950 Dixie Hwy.
Louisville 40216
502-447-7665

Spencerian Collage
P.O. Box 16418
4627 Dixie Hwy.
Louisville 40216
502-447-1000

Owensboro Junior College of Business
1515 East 18th St.
Owensboro 42303
502-926-4040

Kentucky College of Business
198 South Mayo Trail
Pikeville 41501
606-432-5477

Kentucky College of Business
139 Killarney Ln.
Richmond 40475
606-623-8956

LOUISIANA
Baton Rouge School of Computers
9255 Interline Ave.
Baton Rouge 70809-1971
504-923-2525

Delta School of Business & Technology
517 Broad St.
Lake Charles 70601
318-439-5765

Herzing College of Business &
Technology
201 Evans Rd., Suite 400
New Orleans 70123
504-733-0074

American School of Business
702 Professional Dr. N.
Shreveport 71105
318-798-3333

MAINE
Mid-State College
88 East Hardscrabble Rd.
Auburn 04210
207-783-1478

Mid-State College
218 Water St.
Augusta 04330
207-623-3962

Beal College
629 Main St.
Bangor 04401
207-947-4591

Andover College
901 Washington Ave.
Portland 04103
207-774-6126

Casco Bay College
477 Congress St.
Portland 04101
207-772-0196

MARYLAND
Fleet Business School
2530 Riva Rd., Suite 201
Annapolis 21401
410-266-8500

Abbie Business Institute
5310 Spectrum Dr.
Frederick 210701
301-694-0211

Hagerstown Business College
18618 Crestwood Dr.
Hagerstown 21742
301-739-2670

Medix School
1017 York Rd.
Towson 21204-2511
410-337-5155

MASSACHUSETTS
Burdett School
745 Boylston St.
Boston 02116
617-859-1900

Hickox School
200 Tremont St.
Boston 02116
617-482-7655

Katharine Gibbs School
126 Newbury St.
Boston 02116
617-578-7100

Computer-Ed Business Institute
375 Westgate Dr.
Brockton 02401
508-941-0730

Kinyon-Campbell Business School
1041 Pearl St.
Brockton 02401
508-584-6869

Computer Processing Institute
615 Massachusetts Ave.
Cambridge 02139
617-354-6900

Kinyon-Campbell Business School
59 Linden St.
New Bedford 02740
508-992-5448

Computer Learning Center
Five Middlesex Ave.
Somerville 02145
617-776-3500

The Salter School
458 Bridge St.
Springfield 01103
413-731-7353

St. John's School of Business
P.O. Box 1190
West Springfield 01090-1190
413-781-0390

Computer-Ed Business Institute
100 Commerce Way
Woburn 01801
617-933-7681

Burdett School
100 Front St.
Worcester 01608
508-849-1900

The Salter School
155 Ararat St.
Worcester 01606-3450
508-853-1074

MICHIGAN
Ross Technical Institute
4703 Washtenaw
Ann Arbor 48108-1411
313-434-7320

LEARNINGEXPRESS

LEARNINGEXPRESS

20 Academy Street, P.O. Box 7100, Norwalk, CT 06852-9879

FREE! TEN TIPS TO PASSING ANY TEST

To provide you with the test prep and career information you need, we would appreciate your help. Please answer the following questions and return this postage paid survey. As our Thank You, we will send you our "Ten Tips To Passing Any Test" — surefire ways to score your best on classroom and/or job-related exams.

Name : _____

Address : _____

_____

Age : _____   Sex : ☐ Male   ☐ Female

Highest Level of School Completed : ☐ High School ☐ College

1) I am currently :

A student — Year/level: _____

Employed — Job title: _____

Other — Please explain: _____

2) Jobs/careers of interest to me are :

1. _____

2. _____

3. _____

3) If you are a student, did your guidance/career counselor provide you with job information/materials? _____

Name & Location of School: _____

_____

_____

_____

4) What newspapers and/or magazines do you subscribe to or read regularly? _____

_____

5) Do you own a computer? _____

Do you have Internet access? _____

How often do you go on-line? _____

6) Have you purchased career-related materials from bookstores?

_____

If yes, list recent examples: _____

_____

7) Which radio stations do you listen to regularly (please give call letters and city name)?

_____

_____

8) How did you hear about this LearningExpress book?

An ad? _____

If so, where? _____

An order form in the back of another book? _____

A recommendation? _____

A bookstore? _____

Other? _____

9) Title of the book this card came from:

_____

LearningExpress books are also available in the test prep/study guide section of your local bookstore.

LEARNINGEXPRESS

The new leader in test preparation and career guidance!

LearningExpress is an affiliate of Random House, Inc.

Ross Technical Institute
5757 Whitmore Lake Rd., Suite 800
Brighton 48116-1091
810-227-0160

Ross Technical Institute
1553 Woodward Ave., Suite 650
Detroit 48226-2003
313-965-7451

SER Business & Technical Institute
9301 Michigan Ave.
Detroit 48210
313-846-2240

Ross Medical Education Center
1036 Gilbert
Flint 48532-3527
810-230-1100

Grand Rapids Educational Center
1750 Woodworth Northeast
Grand Rapids 49505
616-364-9464

Ross Medical Education Center
2035 28th St. Southeast, Suite 0
Grand Rapids 49508-1539
616-243-3070

Grand Rapids Educational Center
Golf Ridge Center
5349 West Main
Kalamazoo 49009-1083
616-381-9616

Ross Medican Education Center
913 West Holmes, Suite 260
Lansing 48910-4990
517-887-0180

Dorsey Business School
30821 Barrington Ave.
Madison Heights 48071
810-585-9200

Detroit Business Institute–Downriver
19100 Fort St.
Riverview 48192
313-479-0660

Dorsey Business School
31542 Gratiot Ave.
Roseville 48066
313-296-3225

Ross Medical Education Center
4054 Bay Rd.
Saginaw 48603-1201
517-793-9800

Academy of Court Reporting
26111 Evergreen Rd., Suite 101
Southfield 48076
810-353-4880

Dorsey Business School
15755 Northline Rd.
Southgate 48195
313-285-5400

Carnegie Institute
550 Stephenson Hwy., Suite 100
Troy 48083-1159
313-589-1078

Ross Medical Education Center
26417 Hoover Rd.
Warren 48089-1190
810-758-7200

Dorsey Business School
34841 Veteran's Plaza
Wayne 48184
313-595-1540

MINNESOTA
Minnesota School of Business
6120 Earle Brown Dr.
Brooklyn Center 55430
612-566-7777

Duluth Business University
412 West Superior St.
Duluth 55802
218-722-3361

Rasmussen College–Eagan
3500 Federal Dr.
Eagan 55122
612-687-9000

Rasmussen College–Mankato
501 Holly Ln.
Mankato 56001-9938
507-625-6556

Rasmussen College–Minnetonka
12450 Wayzata Blvd., Suite 315
Minnetonka 55305-9845
612-545-2000

Lakeland Medical-Dental Academy
1402 West Lake St.
Minneapolis 55408-2682
612-827-5656

Minnesota School of Business
1401 West 76th St., Suite 500
Richfield 55423
612-861-2000

Minneapolis Business College
1711 West County Rd. B
Roseville 55113
612-636-7406

Rasmussen College–St. Cloud
245 North 37th Ave.
St. Cloud 56303
612-251-5600

Globe College of Business
Box 60, Suite 201, Galtier Plaza
175 5th St. East
St. Paul 55101-2900
612-224-4378

MISSOURI
Metro Business College
1732 North Kings Hwy.
Cape Girardeau 63701
573-334-9181

Sanford-Brown College
12006 Manchester
Des Peres 63131
314-822-7100

Sanford Brown College
355 Brooks Dr.
Hazelwood 63042
314-731-1101

Vatterott College
210 South Main
Independence 64050
816-252-3997

Metro Business College
1407 Southwest Blvd.
Jefferson City 65109
573-635-6600

ConCorde Career Institute
3239 Broadway
Kansas City 64111-2407
816-531-5223

TAD Technical Institute
7910 Troost Ave.
Kansas City 64131-1920
417-883-4060

Metro Business College
1202 East Hwy. 72
Rolla 65401
573-364-8464

Vatterott College
3925 Industrial Dr.
St. Ann 63074-1807
314-428-5900

Sanford-Brown College
3555 Franks Dr.
St. Charles 63301
314-724-7100

Hickey School
940 West Port Plaza
St. Louis 63146
314-434-2212

Missouri College
10121 Manchester Rd.
St. Louis 63122-1583
314-821-7700

Patricia Stevens College
1415 Olive St.
St. Louis 63103
314-421-0949

The Vanderschmidt School
4625 Lindell Blvd.
St. Louis 63108
314-361-6000

Springfield College
1010 West Sunshine
Springfield 65807
417-864-7220

Vatterott College
1258 East Trafficway
Springfield 65802
417-831-8116

MONTANA
Billings Business College
2520 5th Ave. S.
Billings 59101
406-256-1000

May Technical College
1306 Central Ave.
Billings 59102-5531
406-259-7000

NEBRASKA
Grand Island College
P.O. Box 399, 410 West 2nd St.
Grand Island 68802
308-382-8044

Lincoln School of Commerce
P.O. Box 82826, 1821 K St.
Lincoln 68501-2826
402-474-5315

Nebraska College of Business
3350 North 90th St.
Omaha 68134
402-025-7850

Omaha College of Health Careers
10845 Harney St.
Omaha 68154-2655
402-333-1400

NEVADA
Academy of Medical Careers
5243 West Charleston Blvd. #11
Las Vegas 89102
818-896-2272

Las Vegas College
3320 East Flamingo Rd., Suite 30
Las Vegas 89121-4306
702-434-0486

Career College of Northern Nevada
1195-A Corporate Blvd.
Reno 89502-2331
702-856-2266

Morrison College
140 Washington St.
Reno 89503
702-323-4145

NEW JERSEY
Pennco Tech
P.O. Box 1427
Blackwood 08012-9961
609-232-0310

Harris School of Business
654 Longwood Ave.
Cherry Hill 08002
609-662-5300

Dover Business College
15 East Blackwell St.
Dover 07801
201-366-6700

Star Technical Institute
4313 R Rte. 130 S.
Edgewater Park 08010-3105
609-877-2727

Academy of Professional Development
98 Mayfield Ave.
Edison 08837
908-417-9100

Cittone Institute
1697 Oak Tree Rd.
Edison 08820-2896
908-548-8798

Academy of Professional Development
934 Parkway Ave.
Ewing 08618
609-538-0400

American Business Academy
66 Moore St.
Hackensack 07601
201-488-9400

Star Technical Institute
1255 Rte. 70, Suite 12N
Lakewood 08701-5918
908-901-9710

Cittone Institute
523 Fellowship Rd., Suite 265
Mt. Laurel 08054-3414
609-722-9333

Katharine Gibbs School
33 Plymouth St.
Montclair 07042
201-744-6967

RETS Institute
103 Park Ave.
Nutley 07110-3505
201-661-0600

Star Technical Institute
2105 Hwy. 35
Oakhurst 07755-7201
908-493-1660

Business Training Institute
Four Forest Ave.
Paramus 07652
201-845-9300

Computer Learning Center
160 East Rte. 4
Paramus 07652
201-845-6868

Dover Business College
East 81 Rte. 4 W.
Paramus 07652
201-843-8500

Plaza School of Technology
Bergen Mall
Rte. 4 E.
Paramus 07652-9948
201-843-0344

Omega Institute
7050 Rte. 38 E.
Pennsauken 08109
609-663-4299

Katharine Gibbs School
80 Kingsbridge Rd.
Piscataway 08854
908-885-1580

Cittone Institute
100 Canal Point Blvd.
Princeton 08540
609-520-8798

HoHoKus School
50 South Franklin Tpke.
Ramsey 07446
201-327-8877

Star Technical Institute
43 S. White Horse Pike
Stratford 08084
609-435-7827

Berdan Institute
265 Rte. 46 W.
Totowa 07512-1819
201-256-3444

Stuart School of Business
Administration
2400 Belmar Blvd.
Wall 07719
908-681-7200

NEW MEXICO

Metropolitan College of Court Reporting
2201 San Pedro Northeast
Building 1, #1300
Albuquerque 87100-4129
505-888-3400

Parks College
1023 Tijeras Northwest
Albuquerque 87102
505-843-7500

International Business College
650 East Montana, Suite C
Las Cruces 88001
505-526-5579

NEW YORK

Bryant & Stratton Business Institute
1259 Central Ave.
Albany NY 12205
518-437-1802

Mildred Elley
Two Computer Dr. S.
Albany 12205
518-446-0595

Drake Business School
32-03 Steinway St.
Astoria 11103
718-777-3800

Ridley-Lowell Business & Technical
Institute
116 Front St.
Binghamton 13905
607-724-2941

Drake Business School
2122 White Plains Rd.
Bronx 10462
718-822-8080

Bryant & Stratton Business Institute
1028 Main St.
Buffalo 14202
716-884-9120

Utica School of Commerce
P.O. Box 462, Route 5
Canastota 13032
315-697-8200

Long Island Business Institute
6500 Jericho Tpke.
Commack 11725
516-499-7100

Elmira Business Institute
180 Clemens Center Pkway.
Elmira 14901
607-733-7177

New York School for Medical/Dental
Assistants
116-16 Queens Blvd.
Forest Hills 11375-2330
718-793-2330

Bryant & Stratton Business Institute
1214 Abbott Rd.
Lackawanna 14218
716-821-9331

Hunter Business School
3601 Hempstead Tpke.
Levittown 11756
516-796-1000

Bryant & Stratton Business Institute
8687 Carling Rd.
Liverpool 13090
315-652-6500

Katharine Gibbs School
535 Broad Hollow Rd.
Melville 11747
516-293-2460

Blake Business School
P.O. Box 1052
20 Cooper Sq.
New York 10276
212-254-1233

Drake Business School
225 Broadway
New York 10007
212-349-7900

FEGS Trades and Business
17 Battery Pl., 6 North
New York 10004-1102
212-440-8130

Katharine Gibbs School
200 Park Ave.
New York 10166
212-867-9300

The Madison School
500 8th Ave., 2nd Fl.
New York 10018
212-695-2759

New York Institute of Business
Technology
401 Park Ave. S., 2nd Fl.
New York 10016
212-725-9400

Spanish-American Institute
215 W. 43rd St.
New York 10036-3913
212-840-7111

Taylor Business Institute
120 W. 30th St.
New York 10001
212-279-0510

Travel Institute
15 Park Row, #617
New York 10038-2301
212-349-3331

Cheryl Fell's School of Business
2541 Military Rd.
Niagara Falls 14304
716-297-2750

Olean Business Institute
301 North Union St.
Olean 14760
716-372-7978

Utica School of Commerce
17-19 Elm St.
Oneonta 13820
607-432-7003

Krissler Business Institute
166 Mansion St.
Poughkeepsie 12601
914-471-0330

Bryant & Stratton Business Institute
1225 Jefferson Rd.
Rochester 14623
716-292-5627

Bryant & Stratton Business Institute
82 St. Paul St.
Rochester 14604
716-325-6010

Rochester Business Institute
1850 Ridge Rd. E.
Rochester 14622
716-266-0430

Spencer Business & Technical Institute
200 State St.
Schenectady 12305
518-374-7619

Drake Business School
148 New Dorp Ln.
Staten Island 10306
718-980-9000

Bryant & Stratton Business Insititute
953 James St.
Syracuse 13203-2502
315-472-6603

Utica School of Commerce
201 Bleecker St.
Utica 13501-2280
315-733-2307

Business Informatics Center
134 South Central Ave.
Valley Stream 11580-5431
516-561-0050

Westchester Business Institute
325 Central Ave.
White Plains 10606
914-948-4442

Bryant & Stratton Business Institute
200 Bryant & Stratton Way
Williamsville 14221
716-631-0260

NORTH CAROLINA
Cecils College
P.O. Box 6407
1567 Patton Ave.
Asheville 28806
704-252-2486

American Business & Fashion Institute
1515 Mockingbird Ln., Suite 600
Charlotte 28209-3236
704-523-3738

Brookstone College of Business
8307 University Executive Park Dr.
Charlotte 28262
704-547-8600

ECPI College of Technology
1121 Wood Ridge Center Dr.
Charlotte 28217-1989
704-357-0077

King's College
322 Lamar Ave.
Charlotte 28204
704-372-0266

Brookstone College of Business
7815 National Service Rd.
Airport West
Greensboro 27409
910-668-2627

ECPI College of Technology
7015G Albert Pick Rd.
Greensboro 27409-9654
919-665-1400

ECPI Computer Institute
4509 Creedmoor Rd.
Raleigh 27612-3813
919-571-0057

Salisbury Business College
1400 Jake Alexander Blvd. W.
Salisbury 28147-9912
704-636-4071

Miller-Motte Business College
606 South College Rd.
Wilmington 28403
910-392-4660

NORTH DAKOTA
Interstate Business College
520 East Main Ave.
Bismarck 58501
701-255-0779

Interstate Business College
2720 32nd Ave. Southwest
Fargo 58103
701-232-2477

Asker's Business College
201 North 3rd St.
Grand Forks 58203-5876
701-772-6646

OHIO
Academy of Court Reporting
2930 W. Market St.
Akron 44313
216-867-4030

Southern Ohio College–Northeast
2791 Mogadore Rd.
Akron 44312
216-733-8766

Raedel College & Industrial Welding
School
137 Sixth St. Northeast
Canton 44702
330-454-9006

RETS Tech Center
P.O. Box 130
Centerville 45459-6120
513-433-3410

Southeastern Business College
1855 Western Ave.
Chillicothe 45601-1038
614-774-6300

Southern Ohio College
1011 Glendale-Milford Rd.
Cincinnati 45215-1107
513-771-2424

Southwestern College of Business
9910 Princeton-Glendale Rd.
Cincinnati 45246
513-874-0432

Southwestern College of Business
632 Vine St., Suite 200
Cincinnati 45202
513-421-3212

Academy of Court Reporting
614 Superior Ave. Northwest
Cleveland 44113
216-861-3222

MTI Business College
1140 Euclid Ave.
Cleveland 44115-1603
216-621-8228

Remington College
14445 Broadway Ave.
Cleveland 44125-9801
216-475-7520

Sawyer College of Business
13027 Lorain Ave.
Cleveland 44111
216-941-7666

Sawyer College of Business–East
3150 Mayfield Rd.
Cleveland Heights 44118
216-932-0911

Academy of Court Reporting
630 East Broad St.
Columbus 43215
614-221-7770

Bradford School
6170 Busch Blvd.
Columbus 43229
614-846-9410

Akron Institute
1625 Portage Trail
Cuyahoga Falls 44223-2166
216-928-3400

Miami-Jacobs College
P.O. Box 1433, 400 E. Second St.
Dayton 45401
513-461-5174

Southwestern College of Business
225 West First St.
Dayton 45402
513-224-0061

Ohio Valley Business College
P.O. Box 7000
500 Maryland Ave.
East Liverpool 43920
330-385-1070

Stautzenberger College–Findlay
1637 Tiffin Ave., Suite 150
Findlay 45840
419-423-2211

Southeastern Business College
1176 Jackson Pike, Suite 312
Gallipolis 45631
614-446-4367

Southeastern Business College
420 East Main St.
Jackson 45640
614-286-1554

Southeastern Business College
1522 Sheridan Dr.
Lancaster 43130-1303
614-687-6126

Southeastern Business College
1907 North Ridge Rd.
Lorain 44055
216-277-0021

Cleveland Institute of Dental-Medical
Assistance
5733 Hopkins Rd.
Mentor 44060-2035
216-946-9530

Southwestern College of Business
631 South Briel Blvd.
Middletown 45044
513-423-3346

Southeastern Business College
3879 Rhodes Ave., Suite A
New Boston 45662-4900
614-456-4124

ETI Technical College
1320 W. Maple St. Northwest
North Canton 44720-2854
216-494-1214

Bryant & Stratton College
12955 Snow Rd.
Parma 44130-1013
216-265-3151

Bohecker's Business College
326 East Main St.
Ravenna 44266
216-297-7319

Bryant & Stratton College
Sears Bldg., 3rd Fl.
691 Richmond Rd.
Richmond Heights 44143
216-461-3151

Southeastern Business College
4020 Milan Rd.
Sandusky 44870-5894
419-627-8345

Stautzenberger College–South
5355 Southwyck Blvd.
Toledo 43614
419-866-0261

Trumbull Business College
3200 Ridge Rd.
Warren 44484
330-369-3200

ITT Technical Institute
1030 North Meridian Rd.
Youngstown 44509-4017
330-270-1600

OKLAHOMA
School of Technical Training
112 Southwest 11th St.
Lawton 73501
405-355-4416

Metropolitan College of Court Reporting
2901 North Classen Blvd., Suite 200
Oklahoma City 73106
405-528-5000

Wright Business School
2219 Southwest 74th St., Suite 122
Oklahoma City 73159
405-681-2300

Career Point Business School
3138 South Garnett Rd.
Tulsa 74146-1933
918-622-4100

Metropolitan College of Legal Studies
2865 East Skeily Dr., Suite 234
Tulsa 74105
918-745-9946

OREGON
Western Business College
425 Southwest Washington
Portland 97204
503-222-3225

Pioneer Pacific College
25195 Southwest Parkway Ave.
Wilsonville 97070
503-682-3903

PENNSYLVANIA
Allentown Business School
1501 Lehigh St.
Allentown 18103
215-791-5100

Star Technical Institute/Star
Beauty Academy
2101 Union Blvd.
Allentown 18103
610-434-9963

Altoona School of Commerce
508 58th St.
Altoona 16602
814-944-6134

Computer Learning Network
2900 Fairway Dr.
Altoona 16602-4457
814-944-5643

Pennco Tech
3815 Otter St.
Briston 19007-3696
215-824-3200

Computer Learning Network
1110 Fernwood Ave.
Camp Hill 17011-6996
717-761-1481

DuBois Business College
One Beaver Dr.
DuBois 15801
814-371-6920

Churchman Business School
355 Spring Garden St.
Easton 18042
610-258-5345

Allied Medical & Technical Careers
104 Woodward Hill Rd.
Edwardsville 18704
717-288-8400

Erie Business Center
246 West 9th St.
Erie 16501
814-456-7504

GECAC Training Institute
1006 West 10th St.
Erie 16502
814-459-9859

Tri-State Business Institute
5757 West 26th St.
Erie 16506
814-838-7673

Triangle Tech
222 Pittsburgh St., Suite A
Greensburg 15601-9876
412-832-1050

Academy of Medical Arts and Business
279 Boas St.
Harrisburg 17102-2944
717-233-2172

DuBois Business College
1700 Moore St.
Huntingdon 16652
814-641-3689

Cambria-Rowe Business College
422 South 13th St.
Indiana 15701
412-463-0222

Cambria-Rowe Business College
221 Central Ave.
Johnson 15902
814-536-5168

Hiram G. Andrews Center
727 Goucher St.
Johnstown 15905-3092
814-255-8200

Consolidated School of Business
2124 Ambassador Circle
Lancaster 17603
717-394-6211

Star Technical Institute
Oxford Business Center
100 North Buckstown Blvd.
Langhorne 19047
717-829-6960

West Virginia Career College
200 College Dr.
Lemont Furnace 15456
412-437-4600

Newport Business Institute
945 Greensburg Rd.
Lower Burrell 15068
412-339-7542

McCann School of Business
Main and Pine Sts.
Mahanoy City 17948
717-773-1820

Business Institute of Pennsylvania
628 Arch St., Suite B105
Meadville 16335
814-827-0700

Douglas School of Business
130 7th St.
Monessen 15062
412-684-3684

Western School of Health/Business
Career
One Monroe Center
Route 22 & 3824 Northern Pike
Monroeville 15146-2142
412-373-6400

Wilma Boyd Career Schools
1412 Beers School Rd.
Moon Township 15108-2549
412-299-2200

Garfield Business Institute
709 3rd Ave.
New Brighton 15066
412-847-4510

Erie Business Center South
700 Moravia St.
New Castle 16101
412-658-9066

Career Training Academy
703 5th Ave.
New Kensington 15068-6301
412-337-1000

DuBois Business College
701 East 3rd St.
Oil City 16301
814-677-1322

Center for Innovative Training
841 Chestnut St.
Philadelphia 19107
215-922-6555

The Court Reporting Institute
1845 Walnut St.
Philadelphia 19103-4707
215-854-1823

Star Technical Institute
9121-49 Roosevelt Blvd.
Philadelphia 19114
215-969-5877

Thompson Institute
University City Science Center
3440 Market St.
Philadelphia 19104
215-387-1530

Allegheny Business Institute
Investment Building, Suite 617
239 Fourth Ave.
Pittsburgh 15222
412-456-7100

Bidwell Training Center
1815 Metropolitan St.
Pittsburgh 15233-2234
412-323-4000

Bradford School
707 Grant St.
Gulf Tower
Pittsburgh 15219
412-391-6710

Duff's Business Institute
110 9th St.
Pittsburgh 15222
412-261-4520

ICM School of Business & Medical
Careers
Ten Wood St.
Pittsburgh 15222
412-261-2647

Sawyer School
717 Liberty Ave., Suite 800
Pittsburgh 15222
412-261-5700

Triangle Tech
1940 Perrysville Ave.
Pittsburgh 15214-3897
412-359-1000

Western School of Health/Business
Career
421 7th Ave.
Pittsburgh 15219-1907
412-281-2600

Antonelli Medical and Professional
Institute
1700 Industrial Hwy.
Pottstown 19464-9250
610-323-7270

Franklin Academy
324 North Centre St.
Pottsville 17901
717-622-8370

McCann School of Business
101 North Centre St.
Pottsville 17910
717-622-7622

Schuylkill Business Institute
2400 West End Ave.
Pottsville 17901
717-622-4835

Business Institute of Pennsylvania
RD 1, School House Rd.
Pulaski 16143
412-964-0700

Pace Institute
606 Court St.
Reading 19601-3542
610-375-1212

Allied Medical and Technical Careers
2901 Pittston Ave.
Scranton 18505
717-342-8000

Business Institute of Pennsylvania
335 Boyd Dr.
Sharon 16146
412-983-0700

Chubb Institute—The Keystone School
965 Baltimore Pike
Springfield 19064
610-543-1747

South Hills Business School
480 Waupelani Dr.
State College 16801-4516
814-234-7755

Beta Training Services
225 South Chester Rd., Suite 5
Swarthmore 19081
610-543-5000

Laurel Business Institute
11-15 Penn St.
Uniontown 15401
412-439-4900

The PJA School
7900 West Chester Pike
Upper Darby 19082-1926
215-854-1823

Star Technical Institute
1500 Garrett Rd.
Upper Darby 19082
610-626-2700

Penn Commercial College
82 South Main St.
Washington 15301
412-222-5330

Newport Business Institute
941 West 3rd St.
Williamsport 17701
717-326-2869

Berks Technical Institute
2205 Ridgewood Rd.
Wyomissing 19610-1168
610-372-1722

Consolidated School of Business
1605 Clugston Rd.
York 17404
717-764-9550

Yorktowne Business Institute
West Seventh Ave.
York 17404
717-846-5000

RHODE ISLAND
Ocean State Business Institute
Mariner Square, Boxes 1 & 2
140 Point Judith Rd., Unit 3A
Narragansett 02882
401-789-0287

Computer-Ed Business Institute
1270 Mineral Spring Ave.
North Providence 02904
401-722-3520

Nasson Institute
286 Main St.
Pawtucket 02860
401-728-1570

Sawyer School
101 Main St.
Pawtucket 02860
401-272-8400

Johnson & Wales University
Eight Abbott Park Pl.
Providence 02903
401-598-1000

Katharine Gibbs School
178 Butler Ave.
Providence 02906
401-861-1420

Nasson Institute
361 Reservoir Ave.
Providence 02907-3500
401-941-0607

School of Medical and Legal
Secretarial Sciences
60 South Angell St.
Providence 02906-5208
401-331-1711

Sawyer School
1222 Warwick Ave.
Warwick 02888
401-463-3555

Nasson Institute
191 Social St.
Woonsocket 02895
401-769-2066

SOUTH CAROLINA
Columbia Junior College of Business
P.O. Box 1196
3810 Main St.
Columbia 29202
803-799-9082

SOUTH DAKOTA
Nettleton Career College
100 South Spring Ave.
Sioux Falls 57104
605-336-1837

TENNESSEE
Electronic Computer Programming
College
3805 Brainerd Rd.
Chattanooga 37411-3798
615-624-0077

Draughons Junior College
1860 Wilma Rudolph Blvd.
Clarksville 37040
615-552-7600

Miller-Motte Business College
1820 Business Park Dr.
Clarksville 37040
615-553-0071

West Tennessee Business College
1186 Hwy. 45 Bypass
P.O. Box 1668
Jackson 38301
901-668-7240

Knoxville Business College
720 North 5th Ave.
Knoxville 37917
423-524-3043

Nashville College
402 Plaza Professional Bldg.
Madison 37115-4696
615-868-2963

Education America–Southeast College
of Technology
2731 Nonconnah Blvd.
Memphis 38132-2199
901-345-1000

Draughons Junior College
Plus Park Pavilion Blvd.
P.O. Box 17386
Nashville 37217
615-361-7555

Fugazzi College
5042 Linbar Dr., Suite 200
Nashville 37211
615-333-3344

TEXAS
American Commercial College
402 Butternut St.
Abilene 79602
915-672-8495

Austin Business College
2101 IH-35 S., 3rd Fl.
Austin 78741
512-447-9415

Delta Career Institute
1310 Pennsylvania Ave.
Beaumont 77701
409-833-6161

Central Texas Commercial College
P.O. Box 1324
315 North Center
Brownwood 76801
915-646-0521

American Institute of Commerce
9330 LBJ Frwy., Suite 350
Dallas 75243
214-690-1978

Central Texas Commerical College
9400 North Central Expwy., Suite 200
Dallas 75231
214-368-3680

Executive Secretarial School
4849 Greenville Ave., Suite 200
Dallas 75206-4125
214-369-9009

PCI Health Training Center
8101 John Carpenter Frwy.
Dallas 75247-4720
214-630-0568

Business Skills Training Center
325 Pearl St.
Denton 76201
817-382-7922

International Business School
3801 I-35 N., Suite 138
Denton 76205
817-380-0024

Career Centers of Texas–El Paso
8375 Burnham Rd.
El Paso 79907
915-595-1935

International Business College
1030 North Zaragosa Rd.
El Paso 79907
915-859-3986

International Business College
4121 Montana Ave.
El Paso 79903
915-566-8644

Arlington Court Reporting College
901 Ave. K
Grand Prairie 75050
214-647-1607

Bradford School of Business
4669 Southwest Frwy., Suite 300
Houston 77027
713-629-8940

M & M Word Processing Institute
5050 Westheimer, Suite 300
Houston 77056-5608
713-961-0500

Polytechnic Institute
5206 Airline
Houston 77022-2929
713-694-6027

Success Institute of Business
10700 Northwest Frwy., Suite 350
Houston 77092
713-682-2262

Texas School of Business
711 East Airtex Dr.
Houston 77073
713-876-2888

Texas School of Business–Southwest
10250 Bissonnet St.
Houston 77036
713-771-1177

American Commercial College
2007 34th St.
Lubbock 79411
806-747-4339

International Business College
4630 50th St., Suite 100
Lubbock 79414
806-797-1933

International Business School
3300 North A St., Suite 110
Midland 79705
915-684-6960

American Commercial College
2115 East 8th St.
Odessa 79761
915-332-0768

American Commercial College
3177 Executive Dr.
San Angelo 76904
915-942-6797

Career Point Business School
485 Spencer Ln.
San Antonio 78201
210-732-3000

Hallmark Institute of Technology
10401 IH 10 W.
San Antonio 78230-1737
210-690-9000

San Antonio College of Medical and
Dental Assistants
4205 San Pedro
San Antonio 78212-1899
210-733-0777

International Business School
4107 North Texoma Pkwy.
Sherman 75090
903-893-6604

American School of Business
4317 Barnett Rd.
Wichita Falls 76310
817-691-0454

UTAH
Stevens-Henager College of Business
2168 Washington Blvd.
Ogden 84401-1467
801-394-7791

Provo College
1450 West 820 N.
Provo 84601
801-375-1861

Stevens-Henager College of Business
25 East 1700 S.
Provo 84606-6157
801-375-5455

Mountain West College
3098 Highland Dr.
Salt Lake City 84106
801-485-0221

Utah Career College
1144 West 3300 S.
Salt Lake City 84119-3330
801-975-7000

VIRGINIA
Capitol Court Reporting &
Captioning Institute
205 South Whiting St., Suite 608
Alexandria 22304
703-370-2904

National Business College
100 Logan St.
Bluefield 24605
540-326-3621

National Business College
300 A Piedmont Ave.
Bristol 24201
540-669-5333

National Business College
1819 Emmet St.
Charlottesville 22903
804-295-0136

National Business College
734 Main St.
Danville 24541
804-793-6822

Commonwealth College
1120 West Mercury Blvd.
Hampton 23666-3309
757-838-2122

ECPI College of Technology
1919 Commerce Ave., #200
Hampton 23666-4246
757-838-9191

Dominion Business School
933 Reservoir St.
Harrisonburg 22801
540-433-6977

National Business College
51-B Burgess Rd.
Harrisonburg 22801
540-432-0943

National Business College
104 Candlewood Court
Lynchburg 24502
804-239-3500

Phillips Business College
1912 Memorial Ave.
Lynchburg 24501
804-847-7701

National Business College
10 Church St.
Martinsville 24114
540-632-5621

Kee Business College
803 Diligence Dr.
Newport News 23606
757-873-1111

The Braxton School of Business
4917 Augusta Ave.
Richmond 23230-3601
804-353-4458

Commonwealth College
8141 Hull St.
Richmond 23235-6411
804-745-2444

ECPI Computer Institute
800 Moorefield Park Dr.
Richmond 23236
804-330-5533

Dominion Business School
4142-1 Melrose Ave. NW, #1
Roanoke 24017
703-362-7738

ECPI College of Computer Technology
1030 South Jefferson St.
Roanoke 24016-4436
504-342-0043

National Business College
1813 East Main St.
Salem 24153
540-986-1800

Virginia College
2163 Apperson Dr.
Salem 24153
540-776-0755

Washington Business School of
Northern Virginia
1980 Gallows Rd.
Vienna 22182
703-556-8888

Commonwealth College
301 Centre Pointe Dr.
Virginia Beach 23462
757-499-7900

Cooper Career Institute
129 North Witchduck Rd.
Virginia Beach 23462
757-519-9500

ECPI College of Technology
5555 Greenwich Rd., Suite 300
Virginia Beach 23462-6554
804-671-7171

Tidewater Tech
2697 Dean Dr., Suite 100
Virginia Beach 23452
804-340-2121

WASHINGTON
Eton Technical Institute
209 East Casino Rd.
Everett 98208
206-353-4888

Eton Technical Institute
31919 6th Ave. S.
Federal Way 98003
206-941-5800

Eton Technical Institute
3649 Frontage Rd.
Port Orchard 98366
206-479-3866

RCH Technical Institute
500 Southwest 7th
Renton 98055
206-362-2273

American College of Professional
Education
15439 53rd Ave. S.
Tukwila 98188-2338
206-244-3459

Western Business College
6625 East Mill Plain Blvd.
Vancouver 98661
360-694-3225

WEST VIRGINIA
West Virginia Career College
1000 Virginia St. E.
Charleston 25301
304-345-2820

Webster College
412 Fairmont Ave.
Fairmont 26554
304-363-8824

Huntington Junior College of Business
900 5th Ave.
Huntington 25701
304-697-7550

West Virginia Career College
148 Willey St.
Morgantown 26505
304-296-8282

West Virginia Business College
116 Pennsylvania Ave.
Nutter Fort 26301
304-624-7695

Mountain State College
Spring at 16th St.
Parkersburg 26101-3993
304-485-5487

West Virginia Business College
1052 Main St.
Wheeling 26003
304-232-0631

WISCONSIN

Madison Junior College of Business
31 S. Henry St.
Madison 53703-3110
608-251-6522

MBTI Business Training Institute
606 W. Wisconsin Ave.
Milwaukee, WI 53203
414-272-2192

Stratton College
1300 North Jackson St.
Milwaukee 53202-2608
414-276-5200

MBTI Business Training Institute
237 South St.
Waukesha 53186
414-521-3221

PUERTO RICO

Colegio Tecnologico y Commercial
Calle Paz 165 Altos
Aguada 00602
787-868-2688

National College of Business &
Technology
Arecibo Centro Plaza, P.O. Box 4035
Calle M P Aviles Ave V Rojas, #452
Arecibo 00614
787-879-5044

Colegio Mayor de Tecnologia
P.O. Box 1490
Arroyo 00714
809-839-5266

American Educational College
P.O. Box 62
Carretera Num. 2, Km.11 Hm.8
Edificio Federal
Bayamon 00960
787-798-1199

National College of Business &
Technology
P.O. Box 2036 Hwy #2
Ramos Building
Bayamon 00960
787-780-5134

A-1 Business & Technical College
13-14 Dr. Rufo St.
Caguas 00726
787-746-1074

Huertas Junior College
Box 8429
Caguas 00726
787-743-2156

Instituto Vocational y Commercial EDIC
Antiguo Centro Commercial Caguas N.
#8 Esquina 5 Urb, P.O. Box 9120 C N.
Caguas 00625
787-743-0855

Instituto de Banca y Comercio
Box 37-2710, 164 Jose De Diego
Cayey 00737
787-738-5555

National Computer College
P.O. Box 1009
Fajardo 00648
787-863-8918

Atlantic College
P.O. Box 1774
Guaynabo 00970-1774
787-720-1022

Puerto Rico Technical Junior
Ave Ponce De Leon #703
Hato Rey 00917
787-751-0133

Humacao Community College
P.O. Box 8948
Humacao 00792
787-852-1430

Institucion Chaviano de Mayaguez
Calle Ramos Antonini #116 Este
Mayaguez 00608-5045
787-833-2474

Trinity College of Puerto Rico
Box 213 Playa Station
Playa De Ponce 00734-3213
787-842-0000

Metro College
Villa 123
Ponce 00731
787-259-7272

Ponce Paramedical College
L-15 Aracia St.
Villa Flores Urbanization
Ponce 00780-0106
809-848-1589

Electronic Data Processing College
P.O. Box 192303
San Juan 00919-2303
787-765-3560

International Junior College
Building Tartak
1254 Ponce De Leon Ave.
San Juan 00907
787-724-5858

John Dewey College
P.O. Box 19538
Fernandez Juncos Station
San Juan 00910
787-753-0039

Ramirez College of Business &
Technology
P.O. Box 8340
San Juan 00910-8340
787-763-3120

Electronic Data Processing College
P.O. Box 1674, 48 Betances St.
San Sebastian 00685
787-896-2137

MBTI Business Training Institute
1256 Ponce De Leon Ave.
Santurce 00907-3965
787-723-9403

Universal Career Counseling Center
1902 Fernandez Juncos Ave.
Santurce 00909
787-764-0230

CHAPTER | 4

This chapter covers how to get financial aid for the training program of your choice. You'll find information on how to gather your financial records, how to determine your eligibility for financial aid, how to distinguish between the different types of aid, and how to complete and submit your application.

FINANCIAL AID FOR THE TRAINING YOU NEED

By now you've done a lot of thinking about your career goals, and you've decided to consider going to school for training. And somewhere along the way, unless you're independently wealthy and reading this chapter just for fun, financial aid anxiety has reared its hideous, bristly head. But don't despair. This chapter can answer many of your financial aid questions. Also, most schools have good financial aid advisors who can address your concerns and help you fill out the mountain of paperwork.

MYTHS ABOUT FINANCIAL AID

There's a lot of confusion out there about financial aid. Here are some fictions, mostly circulated by the more expensive scholarship search services in hopes you'll pay them a whole lot of money to find information you could dig up yourself. (A search service is okay as a supplement to your own search, but the fee should be under $30, and be warned that you may end up with just with a list.)

Myth #1: Last year, billions of dollars in private-sector aid went unclaimed because students didn't know where to look.

Fact: Most private-sector scholarships are highly competitive, with many more applications than they can possibly approve. Those that go unclaimed tend to be restrictive. A favorite example trotted out by the search services is the award for left-handed students. What the search services don't tell you is that those students who qualify must attend Juniata College in Huntington, Pennsylvania, and that the award is "up to" $1000.

Myth #2: For most students financial aid just means getting a loan and going into heavy debt, which isn't worth it, or working while in school, which will lead to burnout and poor grades.

Fact: Most schools have their own grants and scholarships, which the student doesn't have to pay back, and many students get these; it's also possible to get a combination of scholarships and loans. It's worth taking out a loan to attend the school you really want to attend rather than settle for second choice. As for working while in school, it's true it is hard to hold down a full-time or even part-time job (although you always have the option of attending school half time), but a small amount of work-study employment while attending classes—say 10 hours per week—can improve academic performance because it teaches you important time-management skills.

Myth #3: All the red tape involved in finding sources and applying for financial aid is too confusing to do alone.

Fact: No, it's not. Have some confidence in yourself! If you believe you'll be able to cope with college, you'll surely be able to cope with looking for the money to go, especially if you take the process one step at a time. See the resources at the end of this chapter that you can go to for help.

HOW TO GET STARTED

The main sources of aid available to you are

- private scholarships and grants
- state government financial aid
- federal government financial aid

Keeping these three sources in mind, forget your anxiety, forget the myths, breathe deeply, and take the following first steps.

1. Research the various kinds of aid available to you. The best place to begin is with a visit or phone call to the financial aid office of the school you've chosen or the school you'd like to attend. Ask for all the information available. Your public library reference desk can also help. And don't forget the Internet, but check out the accuracy of the sources of information you find there.

2. Don't be afraid to apply for several kinds of aid at once. For students at two-year or four-year colleges, there is just one application to fill out for financial aid: the Free Application for Federal Student Aid (FAFSA), which you can get, in paper or computer-disk form, by calling the U.S. Department of Education at 800-433-3243. The form is also available at many public libraries and schools. As of this writing, you may fill this form out anytime after January 1 of the year in which you plan to attend school (don't send it in before January 1 or you'll be automatically turned down).

Are You Dependent or Independent?

A dependent student is expected to have a parental contribution to school expenses and an independent student is not. The parental contribution depends on the number of parents with earned income, their income and assets, the age of the older parent, the family size, and the number of family members enrolled in post-secondary education. Income is not only the adjusted gross income from the tax return, but also includes nontaxable income such as social security benefits and child support.

To be classified as an independent student for federal aid purposes, you must:

* be 24 years of age *or*
* married (even if separated the spouse's financial information must be included on the form) *or*
* have a dependent other than a spouse, who gets more than half of his or her support from you and will continue to get that support during the award year *or*
* be a graduate or professional student *or*
* be a ward of the court or an orphan *or*
* be a veteran of the U.S. Armed Forces—formerly engaged in active service in the U.S. Army, Navy, Air Force, Marines, or Coast Guard or as a cadet or midshipman at one of the service academies, released under a condition

other than dishonorable (ROTC students, members of the National Guard, and most reservists are not considered veterans, nor are cadets and midshipmen still enrolled in one of the military service academies)

You do not qualify for independent status just because your parents have decided not to claim you as an exemption on their tax return (this used to be the case but is no longer) or are refusing to provide support for your college education, although student financial aid administrators will sometimes waive this requirement for special conditions—for example:

- if there is dissolution of the family (depending on the circumstances)
- if a legal restraining order has been issued against your parents because of abusive behavior
- if both your parents have been incarcerated
- if your parents live in another country and you have been granted refugee status by the U.S. Immigration Service
- *(sometimes)* if you can prove you are truly self-supporting (some financial aid administrators demand that you have an income of at least $10,000 a year prior to your application to prove your claim)

Gathering Your Financial Records

To fill out the FAFSA or any other type of financial aid application, first gather the necessary financial records. They may include the following documents from you (and your parents, if you're considered a dependent student). The list is not exhaustive, but includes

- U.S. Income Tax Returns (IRS Form 1040, 1040A, or 1040EZ) for the fiscal year that just ended, and W-2 and 1099 forms. However, even though you may not be able to complete your federal income tax return until March or April, you should not wait to file your FAFSA until your tax returns are filed with the IRS. Instead, use estimated income information and submit the FAFSA, as noted below, just as soon as possible after January 1. Be as accurate as possible, but you can correct estimates later.
- Records of untaxed income, such as Social Security benefits, AFDC or ADC, child support, welfare, pensions, military subsistence allowances, and veterans benefits
- Current bank statements and mortgage information

* Medical and dental expenses for the past year that weren't covered by health insurance
* Business and/or farm records
* Records of investments such as stocks, bonds, and mutual funds, as well as bank certificates of deposit (CDs) and recent statements from any money market accounts
* Social Security numbers

Filing Your Forms

File the FAFSA and other forms with the proper institutions *as soon as possible* after January 1 of the year in which you plan to attend school. Make sure you fill out the forms as completely as possible. Obtain certificates of mailing to verify that you sent them.

What Happens Next?

Four to six weeks after you file the FAFSA, you will receive a Student Aid Report (SAR). The SAR summarizes the information you provided on the FAFSA and indicates the amount of Pell Grant (see below) eligibility, if any. It also indicates the Expected Family Contribution (EFC). The determination of financial need depends on two numbers:

* the Cost of Attendance (COA) for your school.
* the Expected Family Contribution (EFC)—the amount of money your family is expected to contribute to your education if you are a dependent student

Your financial need is the difference between the COA and EFC.

SCHOLARSHIPS, GRANTS, AND WORK-STUDY FINANCIAL AID

It just makes sense to check thoroughly into alternate forms of financial aid before applying for a student loan. Set aside some time to look into the grants, scholarships, and college work-study programs available through your school. Making a trip to your prospective college's financial aid office may be all you need to do. Or, as advised above, check out your local library or the Internet.

Scholarships and Grants

Call the financial aid administrator's office at the school of your choice and ask about the college-controlled aid that may be available to you, especially any special merit scholarships. To attract the best students, many schools now offer merit-based aid in addition to need-based aid. Or try calling the Career College Association (contact information is listed at the end of this chapter), which gives scholarships to a limited number of students attending accredited proprietary (private) schools.

Federal Grants

Particularly attractive need-based federal grants are

* the Federal Pell Grant. All college-bound high school students should consider applying for the Pell Grant. In fact, some sources of financial aid require that you apply before you are considered eligible for their program. Pell Grants are awarded only to undergraduate students who have not yet earned a bachelor's or professional degree. Award amounts vary, depending on program funding.
* the Federal Supplemental Educational Opportunity Grant (FSEOG). These grants are for undergraduates with exceptional financial need—that is, students with the lowest Expected Family Contributions (EFC).

Private Scholarships

To find private sources of aid, spend a few hours in the library looking at scholarship and fellowship books or consider a *reasonably priced* (under $30) search service. Make sure the information is up to date. If you're employed, check to see if your employer has aid funds available. If you're a dependent student, ask your parents and aunts, uncles, and cousins to check with groups or organizations they belong to for possible aid sources. For example, any of the following groups may know of money that could be yours:

* religious organizations
* fraternal organizations
* clubs, such as the Rotary or Kiwanas
* athletics clubs
* veterans groups
* ethnic group associations
* unions

Work-Study

As noted above, working part time while in school may actually improve your grades and time management skills, so check with your school's financial aid office for a work program. Look especially carefully into the Federal Work-Study (FWS) Program.

The FWS Program provides jobs for undergraduate students with financial need, allowing them to earn money to help pay education expenses. The program encourages community service work and work related to the student's course of study. You'll earn at least minimum wage and maybe more, depending on the type of work and your skills. The amount of the award will depend on

- when you apply (again, *apply early*)
- your level of need
- the funds available at your particular school

As an undergraduate, you'll be paid by the hour (a graduate student may receive a salary), and you will receive the money directly from your school at least monthly (you cannot be paid by commission or fee). You'll work either on campus for your school, or off-campus for a private nonprofit organization or public agency engaged in "work in the public interest." Students may earn up to the amount of their award at any time during the award period, as long as they do not work more than 20 hours per week. The awards are not transferable from year to year.

Don't forget to check out your student employment office and the classified ads for part-time jobs. I know a woman who ran a dog-walking service one semester and another who had a paper route.

If you cannot subsidize your schooling through scholarships, grants, or work-study exclusively, by all means consider a loan. Be cautious about the amount you borrow, but remember that it's better to go to school than not to.

Student Loans

The first step in finding a student loan is to know the basics. Become familiar with the student loan programs, especially with government loans. Most education loans are available through one of the following programs, in which most accredited colleges and universities participate:

* the Federal Family Education Loan Program (FFELP), in which your bank, credit union, or the school is the lender
* the Federal Direct Student Loan Program (FDSLP), in which the U.S. Department of Education is the lender

There is little difference between these two programs, and your college will help you decide which program applies to you. Other types of loans exist, of course—for example:

* the Federal Perkins Loan, a campus-based low-interest loan funded by the federal government and administered by the school
* other loan programs—private, institutional, and governmental, some regional and some national

Again, your college's financial aid office is the best place to go for details about terms of the loans, whether you must have financial need to receive the loans, repayment schedules, and so forth.

Questions to Ask Before Taking Out a Loan

The main thing is to get the facts and understand clearly the terms of the loan you're about to take out. You'll want to ask the following:

1. What is the interest rate and how often is the interest capitalized? Your college's financial aid administrator (FAA) will be able to tell you this.
2. What fees will be charged? Government loans generally have an origination fee, which goes to the federal government to help offset its costs, and a guarantee fee, which goes to a guaranty agency for insuring the loan. Both are deducted from the amount given to you.
3. Will I have to make any payments while still in school? Usually you won't, and depending on the type of loan, the government may even pay the interest for you while you're in school.
4. What is the grace period—the period after your schooling ends, during which no payment is required? Is it long enough, realistically, for me to find a job and get on my feet? (A six-month grace period is common.)
5. When will my first payment be due, and approximately how much will it be?

6. Who exactly will hold my loan? (As explained below, your loan may be sold by the original lender to a secondary market institution.) To whom will I be sending payments? Whom should I contact with questions or inform of changes in my situation?

7. Will I have the right to prepay the loan, without penalty, at any time?

8. Will deferments and forbearances be possible if I am temporarily unable to make payments? How do I apply for a deferment or forbearance if I need it?

9. Will the loan be canceled ("forgiven") if I become totally and permanently disabled, or if I die?

The Federal Family Education Loan Program (FFELP)

Two types of FFELP loans are

1. Federal Stafford student loans
   * *subsidized*—you must demonstrate financial need; the government pays the interest while you're in school
   * *unsubsidized*—you need not demonstrate financial need; you may have to pay the interest while in school or during deferment periods; the lender may waive this requirement, but in that case the interest will still be added to the principal
   * you may receive both subsidized and unsubsidized loans if you qualify

2. PLUS loans (parent loans)
   * parents need not demonstrate need, but there will be a credit check
   * parents may borrow the full cost of each dependent student's education, minus grants and other financial aid
   * repayment usually begins within 60 days after disbursement

To apply for a FFELP loan, follow the instructions provided by your school in completing the application form. After you fill out your part of the application, the school you plan to attend must complete its part, certifying your enrollment, your cost of education, any other financial aid you'll receive, and in the case of some loans, your financial need.

Then you (or your college) submit the application to the lender.

After the lender approves the loan, a guaranty agency verifies your eligibility and insures the loan for the lender. The lender will send the money (minus the fees mentioned above) to your school, which will contact you.

Loan Repayment

When it is time to repay your loan, you will make payments to your original lender, to a secondary market institution to which your lender has sold your loan, or to a loan servicing specialist acting as its agent to collect payments.

At the beginning of the process, try to choose the lender that offers you the best benefits (for example, lets you pay electronically, offers lower interest rates to those who consistently pay on time, has a toll-free number to call 24 hours a day, 7 days a week). Ask the financial aid administrator at your college to direct you to such lenders.

Be sure to check out your repayment options before borrowing. Lenders are required to offer repayment plans that will make it easier to pay back your loan. Your repayment options will include

- Standard repayment: full principal and interest payments due each month throughout your loan term. You'll pay the smallest amount of interest using the standard repayment plan, but your monthly payments may seem high when you're just out of school.
- Graduated repayment: interest-only or partial interest monthly payments due early in repayment. Payment amounts increase thereafter. Some lenders offer interest-only or partial interest repayment options which provide the lowest initial monthly payments available. Your FAA can tell you which lenders offer the most attractive terms.
- Income-based repayment: monthly payments are based on a percentage of your monthly income.
- FFELP consolidation (available to individual borrowers or married couples): combines any of the following eligible loans—subsidized Stafford, unsubsidized Stafford, PLUS, SLS, Perkins, NSL (Nursing Student Loans), and HPSL (Health Professions Student Loans)—into a single consolidated loan and offers lower initial monthly payments, usually with an extended repayment term. Loan consolidation is not available from all lenders. Prepayment in total or in part is allowed for all federally spon-

sored loans at any time during the life of the loan without penalty. Prepayment will reduce the total cost of your loan.

It's quite possible—in fact likely—that while you're still in school your FFELP loan will be sold to a secondary market institution such as Sallie Mae. You'll be notified of the sale by letter, and you need not worry if this happens—your loan terms and conditions will remain exactly the same. In fact, the sale may give you repayment options and benefits that you would not have had otherwise. Your payments after you finish school, and your requests for information should be directed to the new loan holder.

The Federal Direct Student Loan Program

The Direct Loan Program may also be either subsidized or unsubsidized (see the FFELP section for definitions). The amount you can borrow each year for direct subsidized and direct unsubsidized loans depends on whether you are a dependent or an independent student.

The Direct Loan is more streamlined than the FFELP. Under the Direct Loan Program

- you do not borrow from a bank—the federal government raises the funds through its regular Treasury bill auctions, and repayments are made to the government
- the loans are never sold—repayment is made to the Department of Education for the life of the loan
- you are more apt to borrow only what you need, knowing that if you need more, the funds will be there quickly

Loan Repayment

You may have more flexible repayment options, and you can change options when you need to without a fee at any time during the life of the loan. Repayment options may include

- a standard repayment plan, which requires fixed monthly payments. The length of the repayment period depends on the loan amount. This plan usually results in the lowest total interest paid because the repayment period is shorter than under the other plans.

- an extended repayment plan, which allows loan repayment to be extended over a period from generally 12 to 30 years, depending on the amount borrowed. This plan also results in lower payments each month but much more total interest paid.
- a graduated repayment plan, which allows payments to start out low and increase every two years, generally over a period of from 12 to 30 years. This will be helpful if your income is low initially but will increase steadily. This plan also results in lower payments each month but much more total interest paid.
- an income contingent repayment plan, which bases monthly payments on your income and the total amount borrowed. As your income rises or falls each year, monthly payments will be adjusted accordingly, and you'll have up to 25 years to repay. After 25 years, any unpaid amount will be discharged, but you must pay taxes on the amount discharged.

General Guidelines for All Types of Loans

Before you commit yourself to any loans, be sure to keep in mind that these are loans, not grants or scholarships, so plan ahead and make sure that you don't borrow more than you'll be able to repay. Estimate realistically how much you'll earn when you leave school and remember you'll have other monthly obligations such as housing, food, and transportation expenses.

Once You're in School

Once you have your loan (or loans) and you're attending classes, don't forget about the responsibility of your loan. Keep a file of information on your loan that includes copies of all your loan documents and related correspondence, along with a record of all your payments. Open and read all your mail about your education loan.

Remember also that you are obligated by law to notify both your FAA and the holder or servicer of your loan if there is a change in your name, address, enrollment status (dropping to less than half time means that you'll have to begin payment six months later), or anticipated graduation date.

After You Leave School

Once you leave school you must begin repaying your student loan. This is not necessarily *completely* terrible news. If you have a Stafford loan, you will get a six-month grace period before your first payment is due. Other types of loans have grace periods as well. And if you haven't been out in the world of work before, with your loan repayment you'll begin your credit history. If you make payments on time, you'll build up a good credit rating, and you'll find it easier to get credit for other purchases. Get off to a good start so you don't run the risk of going into default—a terrible, terrible state of affairs that may mean any one or more of the following things will happen.

* trouble getting any kind of credit in the future
* no longer qualifying for federal or state educational financial aid
* having holds placed on your college records
* having your wages garnished
* having future federal income tax refunds taken
* having your assets seized

To avoid the dire consequences outlined above, always be sure to do the following:

* Open and read all mail you receive about your education loans immediately.
* Make scheduled payments on time. Since interest is calculated daily, delays can be costly.
* Contact your servicer immediately if you can't make payments on time. Your servicer may be able to get you into a graduated or income-sensitive/income contingent repayment plan or work with you to arrange a deferment or forbearance. In spite of the horror stories you might hear, the loan officials are pretty nice folks if you don't try to flee your responsibility.
* Notify your servicer about any changes, as noted above; including address changes.

There are very few circumstances under which you won't have to repay your loan. If you become permanently and totally disabled, you won't have to (providing you didn't have the disability before you obtained the aid). Likewise if you die, or if your school closes permanently in the middle of the term, or if you are erroneously certified for aid by the financial aid office. However, if you're simply disappointed in your program of study or don't get the job you want after graduation, you are not relieved of your obligation. I know a student who decided not to pay because "They didn't get me a job like they promised." Since no job was promised to her, ever, that student is in a lot of hot water now.

Remember, too, that there are restrictions on how you can use your loan money. It's to be used strictly for education-related expenses (for example, tuition, fees, books, room and board, transportation, and so on). A CD of your favorite rock band now and then won't hurt, or if you really need a toaster oven you can get by with that. But I know someone who used her loan to buy expensive clothing and a car, then fell so far behind on her school expenses she had to quit. So do watch out.

FINANCIAL AID QUESTIONS AND ANSWERS

Here are answers to the most commonly asked questions about student financial aid:

1. **I probably don't qualify for aid. Should I apply for aid anyway?** Yes. Many families mistakenly think they don't qualify for aid and fail to apply. Remember that some sources of aid are not based on need. The FAFSA form is free—there's no good reason not to apply.

2. **Do I need to be admitted before I can apply for financial aid at a particular university?** No. You can apply for financial aid any time after January 1. However, to get the funds, you must be admitted and enrolled in school.

3. **Do I have to reapply for financial aid every year?** Yes, and if your financial circumstances change, you may get either more or less aid. After your first year you will receive a renewal application that contains preprinted information from the previous year's FAFSA. Renewal of your aid also depends on your making satisfactory progress toward a degree and achieving a minimum GPA.

4. **Are my parents responsible for my educational loans?** No. You and you alone are responsible, unless they endorse or cosign your loan. Parents are, however, responsible for the Federal PLUS loans. If your parents (or grandparents or uncle or distant cousins) want to help pay off your loan, you can have your billing statements sent to their address.

5. **If I take a leave of absence from school, do I have to start repaying my loans?** Not immediately, but you will after the grace period. Generally, though, if you use your grace period up during your leave, you'll have to begin repayment immediately after graduation, *unless* you apply for an extension of the grace period *before* it's used up.

6. **If I get assistance from another source, should I report it to the student financial aid office?** Yes, definitely—and, sadly, your aid amount will probably be lowered accordingly. But you'll get into trouble later on if you don't report it.

7. **Where can I get information about federal student financial aid?** Call 800-4-FED-AID (800-433-3243) or 800-730-8913 (if hearing impaired) and ask for a free copy *of The Student Guide: Financial Aid from the U.S. Department of Education*. You also can write to the Federal Student Aid Information Center, P.O. Box 84, Washington, DC 20044.

8. **Are work-study earnings taxable?** Yes, you must pay federal and state income tax, although you may be exempt from FICA taxes if you are enrolled full time and work less than 20 hours a week.

9. **Where can I obtain a copy of the FAFSA?** Your guidance counselor should have the forms available. You also can get the FAFSA from the financial aid office at a local college, your local public library, or by calling 800-4-FED-AID.

10. **Are photocopies of the FAFSA acceptable?** No. Only the original FAFSA form produced by the U.S. Department of Education is acceptable. Photocopies, reproductions, and faxes are not acceptable.

11. **My parents are separated/divorced. Which parent is responsible for filling out the FAFSA?** If your parents are separated or divorced, the custodial parent is responsible for filling out the FAFSA. The custodial parent is the parent with whom you lived most during the past 12 months. Note that this is not necessarily the same as the parent who has legal custody. The question of which parent must fill out the FAFSA becomes complicated in many situations, so you should take your particular circumstance to the student financial aid office for help.

12. **What do the acronyms on the Student Aid Report (SAR) mean?** You have no doubt noticed that bureaucracies (such as the federal government) just love acronyms. Following are the definitions of some acronyms you'll find on your SAR:

    EFC   Expected Family Contribution
    TI   Total Income
    ATI   Allowances Against Total Income
    STX   State and Other Tax Allowance

EA	Employment Allowance
IPA	Income Protection Allowance
AI	Available Income
CAI	Contribution from Available Income (independent student)
DNW	Discretionary Net Worth
APA	Education Savings and Asset Protection Allowance
PCA	Parents' Contribution from Assets
AAI	Adjusted Available Income
TPC	Total Parents' Contribution
TSC	Total Student's Contribution
PC	Parents' Contribution
SIC	Dependent Student's Income Contribution
SCA	Dependent Student's Contribution from Assets

FINANCIAL AID TERMS—CLEARLY DEFINED

Accrued interest: Interest that accumulates on the unpaid principal balance of your loan

Capitalization of interest: Addition of accrued interest to the principal balance of your loan, which increases both your total debt and monthly payments

Disbursement: Loan funds issued by the lender

Default (you won't need this one): Failure to repay your education loan

Deferment: A period when a borrower, who meets certain criteria, may suspend loan payments

Delinquency (you won't need this one, either): Failure to make payments when due

Forbearance: Temporary adjustment to repayment schedule for cases of financial hardship

Grace period: Specified period of time after you graduate or leave school during which you need not make payments

Guaranty agency: A state agency or private nonprofit institution that insures student loans for lenders and helps administer the FFELP for the federal government

Holder: The institution that currently owns your loan

In-school grace and deferment interest subsidy: Interest the federal government pays for borrowers on some loans while the borrower is in school, during authorized deferments and during grace periods

Interest: The price you pay to borrow money

Interest-only payment: A payment that covers only interest owed on the loan and none of the principal balance

Lender (Originator): Puts up the money when you take out a loan; most lenders are financial institutions, but some state agencies and schools make loans too

Origination fee: A fee, deducted from the principal, that is paid to the federal government to offset its cost of the subsidy to borrowers under the FFELP

Principal: Amount you borrow, which may increase as a result of capitalization of interest, and the amount on which you pay interest

Promissory note: Contract between you and the lender that includes all the terms and conditions under which you promise to repay your loan

Secondary markets: Institutions that buy student loans from originating lenders, thus providing lenders with funds to make new loans

Servicer: An organization that administers and collects your loan; may be either the holder of your loan or an agent acting on behalf of the holder

Subsidized Stafford loans: Loans based on financial need; the government pays the interest on a subsidized Stafford loan for borrowers while they are in school and during specified deferment periods

Unsubsidized Stafford loans: Loans available to borrowers, regardless of family income. Unsubsidized Stafford loan borrowers are responsible for the interest during in-school, deferment periods, and repayment

ADDITIONAL RESOURCES

Telephone Numbers

Federal Student Aid Information Center (U.S. Department of Education)

Hotline	800-4-FED-AID; 800-433-3243
TDD number for hearing-impaired	800-730-8913
Selective Service	847-688-6888
Immigration and Naturalization Services (INS)	415-705-4205
Internal Revenue Service (IRS)	800-829-1040
Social Security Administration	800-772-1213
National Merit Scholarship Corporation	708-866-5100
Sallie Mae's College AnswerSM Service	800-222-7183
Career College Association	202-336-6828

(offers a limited number of scholarships for attendance at private proprietary schools)

Internet Web Addresses

Career College Association: http://www.career.org

Sallie Mae: http://www.salliemae.com

To view the *Student Guide* from the U.S. Department of Education:

http://www.ed/gov/prog_info/SFA/Student Guide

For help in completing the FAFSA:

http://www.ed.gov/pro_info/SFA/FAFSA

To view a list of Title IV school codes used on the FAFSA:

http://www.ed.gov/offices/OPE/14_codes.hml

Financial Aid Books

The Best Resources for College Financial Aid 1996/97

Michael Osborn

Resource Pathways Inc., 1996

> This book provides a path through the forest of information available on financial aid and scholarships. It lists resources available to students, parents, and counselors—books, Web sites, CD-ROMs, videos, software, et cetera—and then recommends the most useful for each stage in the financial aid and scholarship search. It includes a concise description and evaluation of each resource.

College Financial Aid for Dummies

Herm Davis and Joyce Kennedy

IDG Books Worldwide, 1997

> This fun and friendly reference guides readers through the financial aid maze and pinpoints the key elements needed to make the financial aid system work for them. The authors cover the major types of loans, grants, and scholarships available with strategies for how to find and secure them. Cartoon illustrations throughout.

10-Minute Guide to Paying for College

William D. Van Dusen and Bart Astor

Arco, 1996

> A quick, simple, step-by-step guide for getting through the financial aid maze that answers the most pressing financial aid questions. Both parents and students will find spirit-lifting information in this easy-to-use book.

For more listings of Financial Aid and Scholarship books, see Appendix B.

Free Application for Federal Student Aid
1997–98 School Year

WARNING: If you purposely give false or misleading information on this form, you may be fined $10,000, sent to prison, or both.

"You" and "your" on this form always mean the student who wants aid.

Form Approved
OMB No. 1840-0110
App. Exp. 6/30/98

U.S. Department of Education
Student Financial
Assistance Programs

Use dark ink. Make capital letters and numbers clear and legible.   `E X M 2 4`   *Fill in ovals completely. Only one oval per question.*   Correct ●   *Incorrect marks will be ignored.*   Incorrect ⊗ ✓

Section A: You (the student)

1–3. Your name

1. Last name   2. First name   3. M.I.

Your title (optional)   Mr. ○ 1   Miss, Mrs., or Ms. ○ 2

4–7. Your permanent mailing address
(All mail will be sent to this address. See Instructions, page 2 for state/country abbreviations.)

4. Number and street (Include apt. no.)

5. City   6. State   7. ZIP code

8. Your social security number (SSN) *(Don't leave blank. See Instructions, page 2.)*

9. Your date of birth   Month Day Year `1 9`

10. Your permanent home telephone number   Area code

11. Your state of legal residence   State

12. Date you became a legal resident of the state in question 11 *(See Instructions, page 2.)*   Month Day Year `1 9`

13–14. Your driver's license number *(Include the state abbreviation. If you don't have a license, write in "None.")*

State   License number

15–16. Are you a U.S. citizen? *(See Instructions, pages 2–3.)*

Yes, I am a U.S. citizen. ○ 1

No, but I am an eligible noncitizen. ○ 2

A

No, neither of the above. ○ 3

17. As of today, are you married? *(Fill in only one oval.)*

I am not married. (I am single, widowed, or divorced.) ○ 1

I am married. ○ 2

I am separated from my spouse. ○ 3

18. Date you were married, separated, divorced, or widowed. If divorced, use date of divorce or separation, whichever is earlier.
(If never married, leave blank.)   Month Year `1 9`

19. Will you have your first bachelor's degree before July 1, 1997?   Yes ○ 1   No ○ 2

Section B: Education Background

20–21. Date that you (the student) received, or will receive, your high school diploma, either—
(Enter one date. Leave blank if the question does not apply to you.)

• by graduating from high school   **20.**   Month Year `1 9`

OR

• by earning a GED   **21.**   Month Year `1 9`

22–23. Highest educational level or grade level your father and your mother completed. *(Fill in one oval for each parent. See Instructions, page 3.)*

	22. Father	23. Mother
elementary school (K–8)	○ 1	○ 1
high school (9–12)	○ 2	○ 2
college or beyond	○ 3	○ 3
unknown	○ 4	○ 4

If you (and your family) have **unusual circumstances**, complete this form and then check with your financial aid administrator. Examples:
• tuition expenses at an elementary or secondary school,
• unusual medical or dental expenses not covered by insurance,
• a family member who recently became unemployed, or
• other unusual circumstances such as changes in income or assets that might affect your eligibility for student financial aid.

Page 2

Section C: Your Plans *Answer these questions about your college plans.*

24–28. Your expected enrollment status for the 1997–98 school year
(See Instructions, page 3.)

School term	Full time	3/4 time	1/2 time	Less than 1/2 time	Not enrolled
24. Summer term '97	○ 1	○ 2	○ 3	○ 4	○ 5
25. Fall semester/qtr. '97	○ 1	○ 2	○ 3	○ 4	○ 5
26. Winter quarter '97-98	○ 1	○ 2	○ 3	○ 4	○ 5
27. Spring semester/qtr. '98	○ 1	○ 2	○ 3	○ 4	○ 5
28. Summer term '98	○ 1	○ 2	○ 3	○ 4	○ 5

29. Your course of study *(See Instructions for code, page 3.)* [Code] ☐

30. College degree/certificate you expect to receive *(See Instructions for code, page 3.)* ☐

31. Date you expect to receive your degree/certificate   Month ☐ Day ☐ Year ☐

32. Your grade level during the 1997–98 school year *(Fill in only one.)*

1st yr./never attended college ○ 1
1st yr./attended college before ○ 2
2nd year/sophomore ○ 3
3rd year/junior ○ 4
4th year/senior ○ 5
5th year/other undergraduate ○ 6
1st year graduate/professional ○ 7
2nd year graduate/professional ○ 8
3rd year graduate/professional ○ 9
Beyond 3rd year graduate/professional ○ 10

33–35. In addition to grants, what other types of financial aid are you (and your parents) interested in? *(See Instructions, page 3.)*

33. Student employment   Yes ○ 1   No ○ 2
34. Student loans   Yes ○ 1   No ○ 2
35. Parent loans for students   Yes ○ 1   No ○ 2

36. If you are (or were) in college, do you plan to attend that **same college** in 1997–98? *(If this doesn't apply to you, leave blank.)*   Yes ○ 1   No ○ 2

37. For how many dependents will you (the student) pay child care or elder care expenses in 1997–98? ☐

38–39. Veterans education benefits you expect to receive from July 1, 1997 through June 30, 1998

38. Amount per month $ ☐.00
39. Number of months ☐

Section D: Student Status

40. Were you born **before** January 1, 1974? .... Yes ○ 1   No ○ 2
41. Are you a veteran of the U.S. Armed Forces? .... Yes ○ 1   No ○ 2
42. Will you be enrolled in a graduate or professional program (beyond a bachelor's degree) in 1997-98? .... Yes ○ 1   No ○ 2
43. Are you married? .... Yes ○ 1   No ○ 2
44. Are you an orphan or a ward of the court, or **were** you a ward of the court until age 18? .... Yes ○ 1   No ○ 2
45. Do you have legal dependents (**other than a spouse**) that fit the definition in Instructions, page 4? .... Yes ○ 1   No ○ 2

> If you answered **"Yes"** to any question in Section D, go to Section E and fill out **both the GRAY and the WHITE** areas on the rest of this form.
>
> If you answered **"No"** to every question in Section D, go to Section E and fill out **both the GREEN and the WHITE** areas on the rest of this form.

Section E: Household Information

Remember:
At least one "Yes" answer in Section D means fill out the GRAY and WHITE areas.

All "No" answers in Section D means fill out the GREEN and WHITE areas.

STUDENT (& SPOUSE)

46. Number in your household in 1997–98 *(Include yourself and your spouse. Do not include your children and other people unless they meet the definition in Instructions, page 4.)* ☐

47. Number of college students in household in 1997–98 *(Of the number in 46, how many will be in college at least half-time in at least one term in an eligible program? Include yourself. See Instructions, page 4.)* ☐

PARENT(S)

48. Your parent(s)' **current** marital status:

single ○ 1   separated ○ 3   widowed ○ 5
married ○ 2   divorced ○ 4

49. Your parent(s)' state of legal residence [State] ☐

50. Date your parent(s) became legal resident(s) of the state in question 49 *(See Instructions, page 5.)*   Month ☐ Day ☐ Year 1 9

51. Number in your parent(s)' household in 1997–98 *(Include yourself and your parents. Do not include your parents' other children and other people unless they meet the definition in Instructions, page 5.)* ☐

52. Number of college students in household in 1997–98 *(Of the number in 51, how many will be in college at least half-time in at least one term in an eligible program? Include yourself. See Instructions, page 5.)* ☐

Section C: Your Plans *Answer these questions about your college plans.*

Page 2

24–28. Your expected enrollment status for the 1997–98 school year
(See Instructions, page 3.)

School term	Full time	3/4 time	1/2 time	Less than 1/2 time	Not enrolled
24. Summer term '97	○ 1	○ 2	○ 3	○ 4	○ 5
25. Fall semester/qtr. '97	○ 1	○ 2	○ 3	○ 4	○ 5
26. Winter quarter '97-98	○ 1	○ 2	○ 3	○ 4	○ 5
27. Spring semester/qtr. '98	○ 1	○ 2	○ 3	○ 4	○ 5
28. Summer term '98	○ 1	○ 2	○ 3	○ 4	○ 5

29. Your course of study *(See Instructions for code, page 3.)* [Code]

30. College degree/certificate you expect to receive *(See Instructions for code, page 3.)*

31. Date you expect to receive your degree/certificate [Month Day Year]

32. Your grade level during the 1997–98 school year *(Fill in only one.)*

1st yr./never attended college ○ 1	5th year/other undergraduate ○ 6
1st yr./attended college before ○ 2	1st year graduate/professional ○ 7
2nd year/sophomore ○ 3	2nd year graduate/professional ○ 8
3rd year/junior ○ 4	3rd year graduate/professional ○ 9
4th year/senior ○ 5	Beyond 3rd year graduate/professional ○ 10

33–35. In addition to grants, what other types of financial aid are you (and your parents) interested in? *(See Instructions, page 3.)*

33. Student employment   Yes ○ 1   No ○ 2
34. Student loans   Yes ○ 1   No ○ 2
35. Parent loans for students Yes ○ 1   No ○ 2

36. If you are (or were) in college, do you plan to attend that **same college** in 1997–98? *(If this doesn't apply to you, leave blank.)*   Yes ○ 1   No ○ 2

37. For how many dependents will you (the student) pay child care or elder care expenses in 1997–98? [ ]

38–39. Veterans education benefits you expect to receive from July 1, 1997 through June 30, 1998

38. Amount per month $ [ ] .00

39. Number of months [ ]

Section D: Student Status

40. Were you born **before** January 1, 1974? .... Yes ○ 1   No ○ 2
41. Are you a veteran of the U.S. Armed Forces? .... Yes ○ 1   No ○ 2
42. Will you be enrolled in a graduate or professional program (beyond a bachelor's degree) in 1997-98? ..... Yes ○ 1   No ○ 2
43. Are you married? .... Yes ○ 1   No ○ 2
44. Are you an orphan or a ward of the court, or **were** you a ward of the court until age 18? .... Yes ○ 1   No ○ 2
45. Do you have legal dependents (**other than a spouse**) that fit the definition in Instructions, page 4? .... Yes ○ 1   No ○ 2

If you answered **"Yes"** to **any** question in Section D, go to Section E and fill out **both the GRAY and the WHITE areas** on the rest of this form.

If you answered **"No"** to **every** question in Section D, go to Section E and fill out **both the GREEN and the WHITE areas** on the rest of this form.

Section E: Household Information

PARENT(S)

> **Remember:**
> At least one "Yes" answer in Section D means fill out the **GRAY** and **WHITE** areas.
>
> All "No" answers in Section D means fill out the **GREEN** and **WHITE** areas.

STUDENT (& SPOUSE)

46. Number in your household in 1997–98 *(Include yourself and your spouse. Do not include your children and other people unless they meet the definition in Instructions, page 4.)* [ ]

47. Number of college students in household in 1997–98 *(Of the number in 46, how many will be in college at least half-time in at least one term in an eligible program? Include yourself. See Instructions, page 4.)* [ ]

48. Your parent(s)' **current** marital status:

single ○ 1   separated ○ 3   widowed ○ 5
married ○ 2   divorced ○ 4

49. Your parent(s)' state of legal residence [State]

50. Date your parent(s) became legal resident(s) of the state in question 49 *(See Instructions, page 5.)* [Month Day Year 1 9]

51. Number in your parent(s)' household in 1997–98 *(Include yourself and your parents. Do not include your parents' other children and other people unless they meet the definition in Instructions, page 5.)* [ ]

52. Number of college students in household in 1997–98 *(Of the number in 51, how many will be in college at least half-time in at least one term in an eligible program? Include yourself. See Instructions, page 5.)* [ ]

SAMPLE

Section H: Releases and Signatures

Page 4

92–103. What college(s) do you plan to attend in 1997–98?
(Note: The colleges you list below will have access to your application information. See Instructions, page 8.)

Housing codes	1—on-campus	3—with parent(s)
	2—off-campus	4—with relative(s) other than parent(s)

	Title IV School Code	College Name	College Street Address and City	State	Housing Code
XX.	0 5 4 3 2 1	EXAMPLE UNIVERSITY	14930 NORTH SOMEWHERE BLVD. ANYWHERE CITY	S T	XX. 2
92.					93.
94.					95.
96.					97.
98.					99.
100.					101.
102.					103.

104. The U.S. Department of Education will send information from this form to your state financial aid agency and the state agencies of the colleges listed above so they can consider you for state aid. Answer **"No"** if you **don't** want information released to the state. *(See Instructions, page 9 and "Deadlines for State Student Aid," page 10.)* ....104. No ○ 2

105. Males not yet registered for Selective Service (SS): Do you want SS to register you? *(See Instructions, page 9.)* ....105. Yes ○ 1

106–107. Read, Sign, and Date Below

All of the information provided by me or any other person on this form is true and complete to the best of my knowledge. I understand that this application is being filed jointly by all signatories. If asked by an authorized official, I agree to give proof of the information that I have given on this form. I realize that this proof may include a copy of my U.S. or state income tax return. I also realize that if I do not give proof when asked, the student may be denied aid.

Statement of Educational Purpose. I certify that I will use any Federal Title IV, HEA funds I receive during the award year covered by this application solely for expenses related to my attendance at the institution of higher education that determined or certified my eligibility for those funds.

Certification Statement on Overpayments and Defaults. I understand that I may not receive any Federal Title IV, HEA funds if I owe an overpayment on any Title IV educational grant or loan or am in default on a Title IV educational loan unless I have made satisfactory arrangements to repay or otherwise resolve the overpayment or default. I also understand that I must notify my school if I do owe an overpayment or am in default.

Everyone whose information is given on this form should sign below. The student (and at least one parent, if parental information is given) must sign below or this form will be returned unprocessed.

106. Signatures *(Sign in the boxes below.)*

1 Student

2 Student's Spouse

3 Father/Stepfather

4 Mother/Stepmother

107. Date completed

Month	Day	Year
		1997 ○
		1998 ○

Section I: Preparer's Use Only

For preparers other than student, spouse, and parent(s). Student, spouse, and parent(s), sign in question 106.

Preparer's name (last, first, MI)

Firm name

Firm or preparer's address (street, city, state, ZIP)

108. Employer identification number (EIN)

OR

109. Preparer's social security number

Certification: All of the information on this form is true and complete to the best of my knowledge.

110. Preparer's signature Date

School Use Only

D/O ○ Title IV Code

FAA Signature

MDE Use Only
Do not write in this box

Special handle

MAKE SURE THAT YOU HAVE COMPLETED, DATED, AND SIGNED THIS APPLICATION.
Mail the original application (NOT A PHOTOCOPY) to: Federal Student Aid Programs, P.O. Box 4008, Mt. Vernon, IL 62864-8608

THE INSIDE TRACK

Who:	Maritza Murillo
What:	Administrative assistant
Where:	Transpacific Development Company, Santa Monica, California
How long:	One year

Insider's Advice

I worked for a temporary agency called Apple One for a long time before I came to my present permanent job, and I took every opportunity I could to learn about computer software. I'd figure out how to do my job efficiently so that I could take time to experiment on the computer; I learned advanced features such as mail merge, macro writing, and presentation graphics, and I became familiar with WordPerfect, Microsoft Windows, Lotus, and Excel. I've also taken advanced classes in Lotus and WordPerfect. If you apply yourself and learn how the software works in one program, you can work on any program pretty easily. When I first came here, I brought a version of Corel from home and scanned the space plans for each floor of the properties we manage, so that now I can update vacancies for 18 buildings when they're filled. The thing that separates the administrative assistant from the old-style secretary is knowledge of the advanced features of computers.

Insider's Take on the Future

I'm at a point now where I want something more challenging. My goal is to move into a management position. What you need most as an administrative assistant is initiative and flexibility. If you pursue computer knowledge, you're valuable, partly because you make your boss look good! I would advise people going into the administrative assistant field to gain all the advanced computer knowledge they can, then move on into management if they want to.

CHAPTER | 5

In this chapter you'll learn how to land your first job—the job you really want. You'll find practical tips on how to get job-related information, write a resume and cover letter, and ace tough interviews.

HOW TO LAND YOUR FIRST JOB

We all want a good job. We want one that pays well, of course, but also one that we can look forward to going to in the morning. Oh, we won't always be glad to hear the clanging of the alarm, but once we've had our coffee....

In order to get that good job, there are a few basics to master. You should

- formulate a job objective that meshes with your life goals
- conduct a job search, using all available resources
- write a resume
- write a cover letter to go with the resume
- interview successfully
- follow up on the interview

WHAT KIND OF JOB DO YOU REALLY WANT?

A "good job" means something different to everyone. In formulating your job objective, it's extremely important—as it is in all areas of life—to figure out first what *you* want, not what you think you *should* want. Maybe your aim is to someday be executive secretary to the CEO of a multinational organization. Or maybe you're a parent or an artist, and you want a job that's satisfying but that does not consume your every waking moment. Maybe you want to begin as an administrative assistant in a certain field and then move on to an executive position.

Or perhaps you're not sure. If that's the case, before you begin your job search, take a little time to decide what your long-term and short-term goals are. This isn't easy. Here's some advice on goal-setting.

- **Write down** your long-term and short-term goals, rather than just fuzzily formulating them in your mind (long-term goals are measured in years, short-term goals in weeks or months).
- Your goals should describe **in detail** what you want to accomplish, in the long term and in the short term.
- Your goals should be **measurable**, formulated in terms that can clearly be evaluated.
- Your goals should be **challenging**, and they should take energy and discipline to accomplish. If you make things too easy, you'll be bored all your life.
- Your goals should be **realistic** and attainable.
- Your goals should have a definite **point of completion** (long-term life goals should be broken up into short-term goals with definite target completion dates).

In all this careful planning, however, it's important to keep in mind that goals, no matter how carefully formulated, can be changed. Be flexible.

One of the jobs I enjoyed most in my life was the last job I'd ever have thought I wanted, in the statistics department of a Midwestern university. My math skills are atrocious, and I never thought of statistics as anything but stultifying; however, the office was congenial, and after awhile I started to take pride in typing huge equations, margin to margin, with subscripts and superscripts and Greek letters. (This was in the days of the IBM Selectric. I'm sure it's easier now, on a computer, but back then it was an extremely challenging task.) I even enjoyed answering the phone and talking to faraway statisticians who were reviewing articles written by professors in our department. (It turns out that statisticians have some of the best senses of humor I've ever encountered.)

So do your very best to formulate clear goals, but if at first you don't get the job you have your heart set on, remember that you may find an ideal one where you least expect it.

WHAT'S THE BEST WAY TO CONDUCT A JOB SEARCH?

To conduct an effective job search, you need two things: motivation and useful information. The motivation is up to you. Useful information is all around you. Following are some tips for conducting your job search.

- If you're in school, make use of your college's placement office—this is your first and best resource.
- Research the field—go to the library and read professional journals, trade magazines, and industry publications related to the kind of place you think you'd like to work.
- Look at the classified ads daily—apply *immediately* for jobs that catch your eye. If relocating is a possibility, look in out-of-town newspapers as well as local ones (major city newspapers can almost certainly be found in your hometown library).
- Use the Internet's online resources. If you don't have a computer, try your local public library, or if you're in school, your computer lab, to see if it offers Internet access. You can gather research on prospective employers, scan want ads from major newspapers, and apply for jobs right on the Internet. See Appendix B for job-related Web site addresses.
- Call job hotlines—many large organizations maintain a list of job openings through them. Look for the book *The National Job Hotline Directory* (updated annually) to find a list of hotlines near you.
- Use public and private employment agencies (remember that private agencies often charge fees—check out the cost before signing anything).
- Use community nonprofit agencies that offer counseling and training.
- Apply directly to companies or organizations that interest you—you can find plenty in the Yellow Pages, in Chamber of Commerce bulletins, and in other directories.
- Conduct information interviews with people who already work as secretaries or administrative assistants to get inside information, advice, and interviewing practice.
- Check civil service announcements (federal, state, local) for job openings.

- Call labor unions and visit those that represent employees in the kind of business you'd like to work for.
- Contact professional associations (state and local chapters) for leads.
- "Try out" jobs you think you might like by working as a temp.

Networking and Temporary Agencies

Two methods of job-hunting deserve further discussion: networking and temping. These methods are interconnected; the people you meet as a temp may be those who are most important to your job-search efforts.

Networking

Regarding networking, the authors of the *Complete Office Handbook*, a publication of Professional Secretaries International, write: "It is estimated that up to 90 percent of jobs are filled by word of mouth." (I got my current job—which includes writing this book—by networking with a former editor.) Following are some people you can involve in your job-search network:

- friends and relatives
- current or past coworkers or fellow students
- former teachers
- people you meet at meetings or at parties
- the insurance salesperson who comes to call
- secretaries at various offices you may visit on personal business
- people who work for a company you'd like to work for (the *Complete Office Handbook* recommends finding out where such people go for lunch or after work, although it doesn't tell how to hook up with them—perhaps you can think of a creative way)
- people you meet on jobs you get through a temporary agency

You also can network with friends and acquaintances of the people you contact to expand your network base outward. You might land a job through someone who's related to a friend of your aunt's broker—the connection could be long and varied, so keep pursuing new contacts all the time from each contact you make. Follow up with any networking contacts who give you good job leads or access to additional contacts. Send them thank-you notes or zip off a quick email to let them know you appreciate their help.

Temporary Agencies

Temping is an excellent job-search method. Temporary agencies can open the door not only to training but to full-time work as well. Even if you haven't attended secretarial school, all you need to begin is a typing speed of 40 words per minute, a talent for organization, and a sense of how to dress and behave in a business office. As discussed in chapter one, temporary agencies provide excellent interactive computer training programs as well as tips on the proper protocol for doing office work.

Kelly Services has a program called KellySelect, a temporary-to-hire service that lets employers evaluate a candidate's performance during a 90-day trial assignment before making a hiring decision. While at work during the 90 days, the worker receives excellent on-the-job training. The employer has the option, as well, of hiring the candidate immediately if he or she appears especially qualified. KellySelect is also a direct placement service. An employer contracts with Kelly Services to find a candidate for a particular job. Kelly then acts as a kind of human resources agency for that employer, finding a candidate that meets that employer's needs for direct hire.

The only down side to temporary work is that it is tempting to stay in it out of inertia rather than out of love of the lifestyle. If you find yourself fed up with going to a different workplace every week, month, or six months, it's time to seek a permanent job.

But for some people, staying with a temporary job permanently, strange as that sounds, is ideal. Temporary agencies now offer benefits to go along with the variety and flexibility inherent in the work. In chapter one you heard from Byron and Valerie Demmer, who have enjoyed 15 years of temporary office work while traveling and pursuing outside interests. And in the October 1997 issue of *The Secretary*, a magazine published by Professional Secretaries International, temporary office professional Maureen Decola Harrison says

> I'm a temporary employee. I'm not between jobs or trying to decide what I want to do with my life. I have a college degree in clothing and textiles, but it took me only a year to realize that retail wasn't what I wanted to do…. [Temporary employment] keeps work interesting. Every new assignment is an exciting opportunity to meet new people and learn new things.

Temporary work offers challenge, Maureen points out, as well as some say over when she works and when she doesn't. And if she ever does want to go into permanent work, she's in the right place. "I've been offered seven jobs since I started working as a temporary employee [three years ago]," she says. However, she enjoyed the "flexibility, benefits, and challenges" of temporary work too much to accept.

Researching Your Prospective Employer

Remember that any job search is a two-way street: Just as you'll undergo a background check by the company or organization you apply to work for, so should you do a background check on your prospective employer. When you decide to apply for a particular job, or if you know a company or organization you'd particularly like to work for, research the job and the company or organization. Following are some questions to ask.

1. What is the organization's financial condition? If you're interested in a for-profit concern, information on growth prospects for the industry that the company represents is important.
2. Is the organization's business or activity in keeping with your own interests and ethics? Obviously, it is easier and more pleasant to go to work if you are enthusiastic about what the organization does.
3. How will the size of the organization affect you? Large firms generally offer a greater variety of training programs and career paths, more levels to advance to, and better employee benefits than small firms. Large employers may also have better facilities and equipment. However, jobs in large companies are often very specialized, whereas jobs in small companies may offer more variety and responsibility, a closer working relationship with management, and a chance to see your contribution to the success of the organization.
4. Should you work for a new small company or organization or for one that is well established? New small businesses have a high failure rate, but for many people, the excitement of getting in on the ground floor and helping to create the business or organization, and the potential for sharing in its success, makes up for the risk of job loss.
5. Is the organization in an industry with favorable long-term prospects? The most successful firms tend to be in industries that are growing rapidly.

6. Where is the job located? If it is in another city, is the cost of living higher than you're used to? What about the availability of housing and transportation, and the quality of educational and recreational facilities in the new location? Will there be excessive commuting time?

Getting Company Information

It's fairly simple to get background information on a company from the company itself. Try telephoning its public relations office and asking for information. You may receive a copy of the company's annual report to the stockholders, which describes its corporate philosophy, history, products or services, goals, and financial status. Most government agencies, at least, will furnish reports that describe their programs and missions, and many private concerns will as well. Press releases, company newsletters or magazines, and recruitment brochures also can be helpful.

Background information on the organization may be available at your public or school library. If you cannot get an annual report, check the library for reference directories that provide basic facts about the company, such as earnings, products and services, and number of employees. Some directories that are widely available in libraries include the following:

Dun & Bradstreet's Million Dollar Directory
Standard and Poor's Register of Corporations
Directors and Executives
Moody's Industrial Manual
Thomas' Register of American Manufacturers
Ward's Business Directory

Stories in magazines and newspapers can reveal a great deal about a company. You can identify articles about a particular company by looking under its name in periodical or computerized indexes such as those on the list that follows. (Don't bother looking back more than two or three years, though. Things change.) Indexes to periodicals that you'll find in the library include:

Business Periodicals Index
Reader's Guide to Periodical Literature
Newspaper Index
Wall Street Journal Index
New York Times Index

In addition to looking up the company name in periodical indexes and getting information directly from the company, your research might also include:

- looking in trade journals, or company newsletters if you can get them
- writing to the company itself, simply asking for information
- dropping in on various companies, asking questions, and looking around

Using these methods, you can find important information, such as the following:

- amount of pay and quality of benefits compared to market norms
- level of formality and flexibility in the workplace culture
- whether there are training programs available to help employees upgrade their skills
- promotion and raise policies and track records
- level of "family friendliness" (flex time for children's doctor's visits, whether child care facilities are available on the premises, and so forth)
- substantiated complaints against the company
- awards won by the company

Once you have a good idea of what kind of job would suit you best and what company or organization you'd like to work for, it's time for the second and third steps: creating a resume tailored to that job and preparing to ace the interview.

WHAT GOES INTO A RESUME?

The resume is the means by which most employers obtain a written history of the skills, knowledge, and work experience of potential job candidates. Its aim is to get you an interview, not to get you a job. Employers don't hire on the basis of a resume, but unless you prepare a good resume you may never get a chance to pitch yourself to the people you want to work for.

In your resume, you will summarize your employment history and your qualifications for the job you're seeking. A resume is nearly always required for managerial, administrative, professional, or technical positions and is required more and more often for secretarial/administrative assistant positions. Although resumes can be created in a variety of formats, all resumes should contain the following information:

- name, address, and telephone number
- employment objective—the type of work or specific job you're looking for

- experience, paid or volunteer (if applicable)—job title, name and address of employer, and dates of employment
- description of duties you performed on your previous job(s)
- education, including school name and address, dates of attendance, highest grade completed or type of certification, diploma, or degree awarded
- special skills, knowledge of machinery or computer programs, proficiency in foreign languages, honors and awards you may have received
- membership in organizations pertinent to the job you want
- either a list of references or the phrase "references available upon request"

Regarding references, the prospective employer will probably require three of them. Always get permission from people before using their names, and make sure they'll give you a good reference. Try to avoid using relatives as references. For each reference, provide a name, address, telephone number, and job title.

Here are a few additional suggestions for preparing your resume:

Resume Tips

- Prepare several versions, emphasizing skills the various companies or organizations you're applying to are looking for.
- Prepare a resume for people to review and a resume that can be scanned by a computer—the differences are discussed in more detail below.
- Be positive and confident in your resume, but don't lie or embellish heavily—this can lead to disaster later on.
- Don't include your age, race, or ethnic group, or a picture of yourself.
- Don't be flashy or ostentatious—that is, don't use wildly varying fonts and brightly colored paper or ink.
- Don't include the reason you left your last job, no matter how good the reason was—this will be covered in the interview if the company is interested.

What's the Best Way to Organize a Resume?

There are many ways of organizing a resume, but the two major types are

- the chronological format
- the skills format

In the chronological format, you list the dates of your past employment in chronological order. This is a good format for people who have continuous work experience with little or no breaks in between jobs.

In the skills format, you list your skills or qualifications without emphasis on dates of employment. This format is good for people who have been absent from the work force or who have large gaps in employment.

Depending on the job you are applying for, you should choose the format that best highlights your training, experience, and expertise. Take a look at the sample resumes at the end of this chapter. Other examples can be found in publications available through your public library or placement office.

Resumes are screened by two methods: by a person or by a computer.

Resumes Screened by a Person

Resumes to be screened by a person can be a little more varied in terms of layout than those to be scanned by a computer, but you still should not get carried away. The best guidelines:

+ Use no more than two or three fonts and type sizes—10 and/or 12 point, preferably.
+ Do not vary type styles too widely—some variation is good, to make the resume look interesting on the page, but be fairly conservative.
+ Use wide margins (at least an inch all around, preferably more).
+ Select white, off-white, beige, or gray 20-lb. paper.
+ Print in crisp black ink, preferably on a laser printer.

Resumes Scanned by a Computer

The guidelines for an optically scannable resume are a bit more restricted. You can format your resume chronologically or by skills, but be sure to use the following guidelines (certain things confuse a computer that would not confuse a person):

+ Left-justify the entire document.
+ Use a Helvetica, Futura, Optima, Universe, Times New Roman, Palatino, New Century, Schoolbook, or Courier font—10 to 14 point size.
+ Don't adjust the spacing.
+ Avoid italics, script, underlining, columns, newsletter layout, or graphics—boldface is okay.

- Use boldface and/or all capital letters for section headings (but make sure the letters don't touch each other).
- Avoid tabs.
- Avoid light type and dark paper.
- Avoid horizontal lines, parentheses, and brackets.
- Select off-white, beige, or gray 20-lb. paper.
- Print in crisp black ink on a laser printer—do *not* send a fax or a photo-copy.
- Use a paper clip, not a staple, to hold pages together.

Note the section called "Keywords" in the sample scannable resume at the end of the chapter. The computer will be looking for your skills, so you want to make references to them easy to find. The computer won't be as sensitive to your writing style as a human being would be (don't slack on style, though—you're hoping a person will read your words someday!), but it'll be pleased as punch by keywords. Make sure the keywords are concrete. Avoid vague descriptions such as "responsible for training"—instead say, "trained clerks on Microsoft Windows 6.0." The computer just loves specific words (especially nouns, although it'll warm up to the right adjectives, too). Some examples of keywords are:

Taylor Business Institute (name of school)

legal assistant

B.A. degree

Professional Secretaries International

Certified Professional Secretary

CPS (the computer will understand acronyms if they're specific to the profession)

French (language fluency)

Chicago (location)

Lotus 1-2-3

spreadsheet software

organized and dependable

responsible

energetic

When creating a scannable resume, you can use more than one page. The computer can handle two or three, and it won't get bored or irritated at having to slog through the pages, or be hungover from a party the night before, as a human reader (even a big-time executive) might. And the more skills you put in the resume, the more "hits" you'll get from the computer (a "hit" occurs when one of your skills matches what the computer is looking for).

Whether you're creating a scannable resume or one to be read by a human being, you should always take the latter with you to an interview. Human readers will appreciate the formatting you put into it.

How Long Should the Resume Be?

The length and variety of your work experience is your best guide to your resume's length, but one page is generally preferred for a resume to be read by a human being (never make it longer than two). As noted above, a scannable resume can be more than one page, although if you find yourself with over three pages, you may be padding or being wordy or vague. Length as a substitute for work experience may distract from your accomplishments and skills. Here are some guidelines:

* Leave out fluff and other information not directly related to the job you're seeking.
* Don't include information that relates to your personal life—besides being inappropriate, it adds clutter.
* Bulleted statements are good if you can work them in, because they're easier to read.

Following is a list of skills almost any company or organization—from a Manhattan brokerage firm to a small branch library in Dayton, Ohio—will want in a secretary/administrative assistant, so any that you can include on your resume will give you an edge:

* basic knowledge of computers—ability to use the latest software programs: word processing, databases, and spreadsheets
* good keyboard skills
* ability to compose effective business correspondence and reports
* ability to relay messages accurately orally or in writing, and to give clear instructions to others
* ability to produce accurate and correctly spelled documents from a transcriber
* ability to understand organizational relationships, roles, and functions

* ability to work independently, solve problems, and make decisions
* willingness to take instruction
* ability to take rapid notes and reproduce documents from those notes
* good telephone skills
* strong editing and proofreading skills
* ability to plan business trips and activities

When you've finished writing your resume, ask someone you trust to read it and suggest ways to improve it.

Always include a brief cover letter with your resume, introducing yourself and saying what type of job you're applying for and, briefly, why.

What Goes in a Cover Letter?

A cover letter is a way to introduce yourself to employers. It should be brief and capture the employer's attention, but it should not repeat too much of what is in the resume. It should not be cute or boastful. It should follow a business-letter format and should generally include the following information:

* the name and address of the specific person to whom the letter is addressed
* the reason for your interest in the company or position
* your main qualifications for the position (in brief)
* a request for an interview
* your phone number

See the sample cover letter at the end of this chapter.

THE INTERVIEW

An interview gives you the best opportunity to show an employer your qualifications, so it pays to be well prepared. Each interview is different; however, following are some suggestions that will fit any situation:

* Prepare carefully—learn as much as you can about the organization you're interviewing with.
* Make sure you have the skills and/or experience required for the job.
* Practice your interview with a friend or relative.
* Try to appear relaxed—it's easiest to if you get enough sleep the night before and are prepared when you go in.

- Be well-groomed—dress neatly and fairly conservatively (although a touch of bright color somewhere won't hurt).

- Arrive a little ahead of time—before the day of the interview, know where the company is located, and leave yourself enough time to find the exact office.

- Learn the name of your interviewer and shake hands when you meet.

- During the interview, make eye contact; speak up and speak clearly; don't slouch; do not chew gum or smoke.

- Use proper English and avoid slang.

- Answer each question concisely—don't ramble.

- If you're asked about a skill you don't possess, admit it, but say you're willing to learn.

- Ask questions about the position and the organization—show enthusiasm and genuine interest (if you don't have either, you should be home in bed).

- Strive for moderation in selling yourself; don't puff yourself up, but don't be too modest, either—it's best just to be honest.

- Know how much money you want or will settle for, but let the prospective employer bring up the subject of money first.

- Thank the interviewer, and follow up with a letter.

Interviews are usually scary, but here's something to remember: You're interviewing the company as much as it is interviewing you. As you're led through the office, look around; note the employees' dress and body language; note the interviewer's dress and body language. Keep your eyes open for indications of the atmosphere in the office; note the expressions on people's faces. Does this look like a place where you *want* to work?

At the same time, don't forget what I said early in this chapter about the importance of keeping an open mind. Even if the job isn't exactly what you had in mind, do as well as you can in the interview. If you're offered the job, you can always turn it down. On the other hand, it may turn out to be your dream job.

EVALUATING A JOB OFFER

Oh happy day! You've been offered the job—and maybe you've been offered one or two others you've interviewed for. Now you have to decide—or, even more happily, choose. How should you go about it? Probably the company or organization will not expect you to accept or reject an offer on the spot. You may be given a week or more to make up your mind.

There are many issues to consider when assessing the offer, and somehow you must develop a set of criteria for judging the job offer or offers, whether this is your first job, you're reentering the labor force after a long absence, or you're just planning a change. Here are some aspects of the job to look at carefully before you make your decision.

The nature of the work: Even if everything else about the job is good, you will be unhappy if you dislike the day-to-day work. Determining in advance whether you will like the work may be difficult. However, the more you find out about it before accepting or rejecting the job offer, the more likely you are to make the right choice. Based on what you learned about the job during your initial research and during your interview, ask yourself the following questions:

Does the work match your interests and make good use of your skills? The duties and responsibilities of the job should have been explained in enough detail during the interview to answer this question.

How important is the job to this company? An explanation of where you fit in the organization and how you are supposed to contribute to its overall objectives should give you an idea of the job's importance.

Were you comfortable with the interviewer or with the supervisor you'll have (if you met her or him)?

Is this the kind of atmosphere you'd enjoy day in and day out? As you walked through on the way to your interview, or as you were being shown around, did the other employees seem friendly and happy? Did they seem too happy? (If they were shrieking with laughter and throwing spit-wads, maybe not enough is being demanded of them. On the other hand, maybe this is just what you're looking for.) If possible, find out the company's turnover rate, which will indicate how satisfied other employees are with their job and the company.

Does the work require travel? Some secretaries and administrative assistants do travel, with or without their bosses. How would this fit into the way you live your life?

Does the job call for irregular hours? Sometimes this fact isn't advertised. It's best to find out during the interview, then decide if the hours fit in with your preferred lifestyle. Some jobs require night or holiday work; others routinely require overtime to meet deadlines or sales or production goals, or to better serve customers. Consider the effect of work hours on your personal life. Also, depending on the job, you may or may not be exempt from laws requiring the employer to compensate you for overtime. Find out how many hours you will be expected to work each week and whether you receive overtime pay or compensatory time off for working more than the specified number of hours in a week.

What are the opportunities offered by the job? A good job usually offers you the opportunity to learn new skills, to increase your earnings, and to rise to a position of greater authority, responsibility, and prestige. A lack of opportunity for betterment can dampen interest in the work and result in frustration and boredom. The person who offers you the job should give you some idea of promotion possibilities within the organization. What is the next step on the career ladder? Is it a step you'd want to take? If you have to wait for a job to become vacant before you can be promoted, how long is the wait likely to be? Employers have different policies regarding promotion from within the organization. When opportunities for advancement do arise, will you compete with applicants from outside the company? Can you apply for other jobs in the organization, or is mobility limited?

What are the salary and benefits? As noted above, during the interview, it's best to wait for the interviewer to introduce these subjects. And he or she may not! Many companies will not talk about pay until they have decided to hire you. Once they've made the offer, though, they're bound to mention pay, and in order to know if their offer is reasonable, you need a rough estimate of what the job *should* pay. To get an idea of what the salary should be, talk to a friend who was recently hired in a similar job. If you've just finished school, ask your teachers and the staff in the college placement office about starting pay for graduates with your qualifications. Scan the classified ads in newspapers and see what salaries are being offered for similar jobs. Detailed data on wages and benefits are also available from The Bureau of Labor Statistics, Division of Occupational Pay and

Employee Benefit Levels, 2 Massachusetts Ave. NE., Room 4160, Washington, DC 20212-0001; 202-606-6225. If you are considering the salary and benefits for a job in another geographic area, be sure to make allowances for differences in the cost of living, which may be significantly higher in a large metropolitan area than in a smaller city, town, or rural area. Do take into account that the starting salary is just that, the start. Your salary should be reviewed on a regular basis; many organizations do it every 12 months. How much can you expect to earn after one, two, or three or more years? Benefits can also add a lot to your base pay, but they vary widely. Find out exactly what the benefit package includes and how much of the cost you must bear for, say, medical or life insurance.

Whatever happens, however the above questions are answered, eventually you'll accept one of the jobs you've been offered. When that happens, here's what to do first: Celebrate. Go out to a good dinner with friends, or buy that special something you've been eyeing, or take a walk with your dog on the beach. Then gear up for your first day of work and for your new life.

We'll discuss the challenges of that in the next chapter.

Sample Chronological Resume

Corina Weeble
76 Round Street, Apt. 10
Kansas City, MO 64112
816-555-3944

Job Objective: Administrative assistant in veterinarian's office

EXPERIENCE

1996-present
Paws 'n' Claws Pet Boutique
96 Rosemary Lane
Columbia, MO 65203
Administrative assistant to owner

* Maintained files and records, did light bookkeeping
* Occasionally assisted owner and groomers with animals
* Handled scheduling of all in-town and out-of-town business meetings and grooming demonstrations
* Composed and typed all correspondence

1994-1996
Bob's Friendly Taxi
9 Seymore Place
Iberia, MO 65000
Dispatcher

* Dispatched for three drivers, part time while in high school
* Maintained schedules and time sheets
* Answered phone, relayed messages to owner

QUALIFICATIONS AND SKILLS

Two years of office support and customer relations experience in pet grooming office

Familiar with Windows 3x and Windows 95

Excellent time-management and organizational skills

Excellent written and verbal communications skills

Dependable and self-motivated

Warm, affectionate manner with animals

REFERENCES   Available upon request

Sample Skills Resume

Hamid Al-Jurf, CPS
1916 Papaya Way
Iowa City, IA 52245

Job Objective: Administrative assistant in a physician's office, with patient contact

QUALIFICATIONS

* Eight years of experience as medical transcriptionist in large teaching hospital
* Two years of experience as ward clerk on inpatient neurology ward
* Sound knowledge of medical terminology in the areas of internal medicine and neurology
* Skilled at transcribing from wide variety of dictating and handwriting styles
* Familiar with Windows 3x, Windows 95, Macintosh plus variety of word processing, database, and spreadsheet software
* Excellent keyboarding skills
* Excellent writing and editing skills
* Excellent interpersonal skills
* Consistently earned outstanding employment evaluations
* Earned Certified Professional Secretary (CPS) rating, 1995

PROFESSIONAL EXPERIENCE

* Transcribed medical records from dictation and handwritten copy
* Trained other medical transcriptionists regularly for six years
* Wrote manual for physicians on how to dictate medical records clearly and effectively
* Set up computer time-keeping method for 20 medical transcriptionists
* Did computer software troubleshooting on night shift for two years
* Had extensive patient contact while a ward clerk on inpatient neurology unit

EMPLOYMENT HISTORY

1988-present   *Medical transcriptionist,* University of Iowa Hospitals & Clinics, Iowa City

1986-1988   *Ward clerk on Inpatient Neurology Unit,* University of Iowa Hospitals & Clinics, Iowa City

EDUCATION AND PROFESSIONAL AFFILIATIONS

Associate degree, Medical Secretary Program, Hamilton College, Des Moines, Iowa

Bachelor's degree, General Studies, the University of Iowa, Iowa City

Member of Professional Secretaries International—The Association for Office Professionals

Sample Scannable Resume

Tanya Jacobs, CPS
1450 Dinwiddy Court
San Diego, CA 94555
Telephone: 415-555-9876

Objective
Administrative assistant—responsible position as assistant to upper management in travel agency

Keywords
Microsoft Windows, Excel, Lotus 1-2-3
keyboarding
friendly, energetic, self-motivated
composition expertise
Spanish fluency

Skills
*   proficient in Microsoft Word for Windows, Excel, Lotus 1-2-3
*   excellent keyboarding skills—fast and accurate
*   experienced in customer relations and service—friendly, professional, personable
*   excellent written and verbal communication skills
*   self-motivated, independent worker
*   ability to work well under pressure
*   bilingual—fluent in English and Spanish
*   innovative in developing work-flow systems

Professional Highlights

Wagons West Travel, 1995–present
Denver, Colorado
Administrative assistant
Duties
*   keyboarding itineraries
*   composing and editing correspondence for three travel agents
*   proofreading and editing agency newsletter
*   answering phones for six people
*   maintaining alphabetic and numeric files

Alfred E. Packer Restaurant & Lounge
Boulder, Colorado
Part-time administrative assistant while in college
Duties
*   acted as secretary to the manager
*   keyboarding correspondence
*   keyboarding menus
*   answering phone for manager
*   maintaining alphabetic files

References furnished upon request

Sample Cover Letter

76 Round Street, Apt. 10
Kansas City, MO 64112
May 5, 1998

Abigail Hartebeest, D.V.M.
Hartebeest Animal Hospital & Clinic
1916 Elbow Street
Kansas City, MO 64110

Dear Dr. Hartebeest:

I am very interested in applying for the job as administrative assistant listed in the *Kansas City Star* on May 2, 1998.

As you can see from my enclosed resume, I worked for a pet grooming salon in Columbia for two years prior to moving to Kansas City. I enjoyed the work very much. I'm an organized, detail-oriented person who gets along well with people. I also have a great love of animals. I feel that these attributes, along with my work experience, qualifies me for the position described in your advertisement.

I would greatly appreciate the opportunity for a personal interview. You can reach me at 555-3944.

Thank you for your consideration.

Sincerely,

Corina Weeble

THE INSIDE TRACK

Who: Craig Spitzer

What: Administrative assistant

Where: Dean of Students Office
University of Iowa Law Center
Iowa City, Iowa

How long: 10 years

Insider's Advice

I work in the front office, so I'm responsible for answering questions that students and the public have. I answer phones, type reports and correspondence using WordPerfect for Windows 6.1, and update the Law School calendar of events on Netscape. I do everything from opening the dean's mail and passing on the important pieces, to ordering supplies, to scheduling Law School events using a database computer program. I'm very busy all day, but I don't take work home with me. My advice to people going into the field would be, first, to learn how to prioritize and then reprioritize when there's a crisis that needs attention first. Be yourself, but be adaptable, and if you're dealing with people, learn patience. There are hundreds of students in the Law School, and sometimes I am asked the same question 102 times, but I have to remember that each student who asks really doesn't know the answer. Most students are polite, but some are rude or spoiled, so I have to be diplomatic. The most important skills for the job are people skills and organizational skills. And you have to have computer skills or you probably won't get a job.

Insider's Take on the Future

I used to be a high school teacher, but I didn't feel dedicated to teaching as I knew I should be, so I gave it up. I like my current job, and I intend to stay in administrative assisting, although I will apply to advance to the next civil service level in my field. I make good money and live comfortably. I'm happy in my work.

CHAPTER | 6

This chapter will give you tips on managing relationships with your boss and coworkers and fitting into the particular culture of your new workplace. You'll find out how to find a mentor and how to promote yourself to get ahead.

HOW TO SUCCEED ONCE YOU'VE LANDED THE JOB

Managing work relationships is an important step to becoming successful on your job. There are many myths about gossip, backbiting, and even back*stabbing* among secretaries and other office workers, but the truth is that office workers get along with one another just as well as world leaders do—and therein lies the problem. Just as in the larger world, many of the issues that cause conflict in the office center around control, so as you go about your tasks, the first thing to remember is that you should keep your focus on the work itself, rather than on the office hierarchy. Whether your new job is in a small company or a megaconglomerate, whether it's just you and your boss or there's a hierarchy that would rival a medieval kingdom, your workplace cannot run efficiently without teamwork—between you and your boss and between you and your coworkers.

YOU AND YOUR BOSS

Secretaries and their bosses have a special relationship that some people have compared to a marriage, and in some cases they spend more time together than most husbands and wives. An excellent relationship is a gift, a bad one is a daily nightmare; most fall somewhere in between. Because no two bosses are alike, just as no two secretaries are alike, it's impossible to give advice that will cover every situation; however, there are a few rules that you can apply to this important relationship that will make it more rewarding and conflict-free. According to Kay May, administrative assistant to an executive vice president of American Express Financial Advisors, the most important aspect of a boss-secretary relationship is open communication and trust. She counts herself extremely fortunate to have such a relationship with her boss and credits her 16-year-long, challenging and satisfying job to this relationship. "It's not something that just happens," Kay says. "Both of you have to work at it."

Following are some suggestions to help you start building a cooperative relationship with your boss, providing he or she is rational and motivated in that direction.

Be as clear as possible about what your boss expects.

If you don't have a formal, written job description and you feel even minimally comfortable asking for one, do so. It takes some tact to do this; you should start by explaining why you want one. Don't simply say, "I'd like my job description in writing, please." That sounds like a challenge, or as though you're going to be too lazy to do anything that's not in the description. It's best to say something like "If possible, I'd like to get a list of the duties I'll be performing every day. I know it's not possible to describe everything, but I don't want to leave anything undone that I'm responsible for." If possible, ask at the very beginning of your relationship before any tension has built up, so it won't seem like a challenge to your boss's authority.

If you don't understand your boss's instructions, ask for clarification.

You cannot work effectively if you don't know what's expected of you. If instructions for doing a task are unclear, you must ask for further details. Don't be afraid of appearing stupid. Most bosses would prefer that you ask for clarification rather than try to muddle through and make mistakes.

Be flexible.

If your boss *occasionally* asks you to do something that's not in your job description—as long as the demand isn't unethical (dishonest or sexist, for example)—it's best to go ahead and do it. If you're rigid about what you will and won't do, your boss is liable to become rigid too. If she or he *consistently* expects you to perform tasks outside your job description—things you feel are demeaning, especially—eventually you'll have to say, *very diplomatically,* that you are not comfortable doing them. As to what's demeaning, that's an individual matter. I wouldn't be comfortable getting coffee or lunch for my boss every day, but once in awhile I'd be happy to do it as a favor. On the other hand, if I had a dreamy boss who was respectful of me in every other way, I might work such a chore into my regular schedule without grumbling. Only you can decide, but don't get into a habit that makes you grind your teeth in your sleep.

If you are asked to do something that's outside your job description, do it a couple of times, and then, the next time it comes up, plan to be extremely busy at some other task that *is* within your job description. If your boss isn't a complete dunce, he or she will get the message.

Try to think of ways to make your boss look good.
Remember, from chapter one, the qualities Deborah Conger said she'd look for in a secretary? One of them was "makes me look good." This isn't a Pollyanna kind of thing. If your boss looks good, you look good—the whole team does. And a successful team is a happy team and one whose members keep their jobs.

Don't go over your boss's head for anything but the most dire reasons.
It's not an inviolable rule *never* to complain about your boss to a higher authority. In cases of actual discrimination or harassment, of course you have to go to someone else. But in general it's best to take complaints to your boss first and try to settle the matter privately—give him or her a chance to correct bad behavior or explain policies that seem unreasonable or unclear. This takes courage, but the payoffs are large. You may find there's a reason behind your boss's "unreasonable" behavior that you never even thought of.

Understand that your boss has problems too.
This is easy to forget. When people have authority over you, it's hard to remember that they're just human. They have kids at home who misbehave, cats that need to go to the vet, deadlines to meet, bosses of their own—sometimes bad ones—overseeing their work. If your boss *occasionally* acts unreasonable, try to keep in mind that it might have nothing to do with you. Of course, if his or her behavior is

consistently abusive, you'll have to do something about it—confront the problem or even quit. But occasional mood swings are something we're all entitled to.

The best way to handle demands that aren't horrendous but only annoying—shifting deadlines, for example, or failure to make priorities clear—is to ask your boss for a one-on-one conference to clarify things. If you keep focused during the conference on *the needs of the team* (rather than on who's top dog—in the office, your boss is), it'll probably go smoothly, and your work life (a large chunk of the time you have here on earth) will be more pleasant and rewarding.

YOU AND YOUR COWORKERS

Remember: The important thing to concentrate on is *work* and the needs of the team. This attitude will help keep you focused and will lessen the impact of the inevitable interpersonal tensions that are part of office life.

The main thing is to follow the rules of good ethics, as follows:

Take responsibility for your actions.

Don't blame the company, your boss, or your coworkers for your mistakes; when you're the one in the wrong, own up to it. In a well-run organization, it's not fatal to admit you've made an error. Conversely, don't grovel or say you're wrong when you don't believe you are.

Never take credit for another worker's ideas.

It's just plain wrong, and besides, eventually you'll be found out.

Do not violate confidentiality, whether the company's or a coworker's.

As a secretary or administrative assistant, you'll likely be privy to company or organization information that is confidential. Similarly, you may—especially if you're in a position of authority—be trusted with a personal confidence. Although you may be tempted, do not violate confidentiality in either case, as you can seriously damage the company or organization for which you work, or your relationship to customers, clients, or coworkers.

Refuse to cover up serious wrongdoing.

While violating legitimate confidentiality is always ill-advised, neither should you cover up serious violations of ethics, whether by coworkers, your boss, or even the company or organization itself. "I was just doing my job" is not an acceptable excuse for ethics violations anymore. If you find yourself working for a boss or company with ethics that seriously violate yours, never use the excuse "I'm just a secretary." Even if you can't bring yourself to blow the whistle (and whistle-blowing, though it may be the right thing to do, can have horrible consequences), at least start looking for another job. You'll feel better about yourself and about the world.

Help others, especially new employees.

Help your coworkers if they need it. (Of course, don't meddle or step in when you sense your help isn't wanted.) Give new employees extra support. Especially important are the seemingly little things—telling a new secretary or clerk when it's time for coffee breaks, if someone else didn't do that, or showing the way to the employee lounge and restrooms. We're all familiar with that sweaty-palmed feeling of the first day of work, even the first weeks of work. Remember what it's like to be new, and empathize.

Be positive about others' achievements.

Never undermine anyone in your office by devaluing their achievements, even if their "achievements" seem minor or dishonest. Don't be afraid that another person will look better than you. In a good workplace, one in which teamwork is valued, there's room for everyone to look good, and slackers will be found out.

Do not complain to the boss about a coworker's behavior.

Do not complain to your boss about another person's behavior, except when the matter is *extremely* serious. Unless the behavior of a coworker is really egregious, try every other avenue to resolve the situation before complaining to your boss. If a coworker is committing infractions that violate important ethical rules (consistent sexist or racist treatment of other employees would be an example) or that violate confidentiality or otherwise damage the company or its customers, of course a complaint is in order. But for lesser matters—especially for interpersonal conflicts—complaints to the boss, reminiscent of tattling in grade school, have a way of backfiring. It's best to talk to the person involved, or, if it's something minor, simply to ignore the behavior.

Don't engage in destructive gossip.

Secretaries have an undeserved reputation as gossips; the truth is, executives gossip just as much. Still, you don't want to perpetuate the myth. A little gossip is inevitable, of course. Someone's bound to bring up the topic of whether Blair's girlfriend *really* knows Tom Cruise, or what on earth Sarah was thinking when she went out with Roger, considering he's still in that body cast. If you never gossip, you'll get a reputation as one of those prim and prudish sticks of a secretary whom people make fun of.

If the talk turns really vicious, however, it's best to gracefully drift away, or suddenly be overcome by the need for peanut M&Ms, which are in the vending machine way over on the other side of the breakroom. Gossip's fun in moderation, but really, very little of it is truly harmless, and there's always the chance that it's untrue.

If you're put in charge, don't overstep your authority.

If you're promoted to a position of authority—office manager, say—don't turn into a rotten boss yourself by overstepping your boundaries. By the same token, don't *under*step—don't do everything yourself, if part of your job is to delegate responsibility. You may think you're just being responsible and hardworking, but your coworkers may take it as grandstanding. And remember, as a supervisor it's just as important to know exactly what's expected of you as it is when you are in a single-person office. Find out from your boss just what the limits of your authority are.

When conflicts arise, attack the problem, not the other person.

If the secretary in the billing department is consistently late getting invoices to you, making you work late, wait for a day when you're feeling good—when you got enough sleep the night before and have something pleasant planned for that evening—and then talk to him or her, keeping the focus on how the problem affects your life, not on what a terrible person the other secretary is. *Don't* suddenly, after months of biting your tongue, storm into her or his office shrieking. Instead, just as you would with your boss, ask for a one-on-one conference, and keep the good of the team uppermost in your mind. Remember: attack the problem, not the person. And rather than focusing on how the other person is doing his or her job, you may get better results by emphasizing the problem's effects on your personal life.

Instead of saying, "It's *your* responsibility to see the invoices get to me on time. How am I supposed to do my job, anyway? From now on, do it right," say something like, "Could we work something out about the timing of the invoice delivery? My husband/wife (dog/cat/bird) really gets upset with me when I stay late at work."

If the other person ignores your request, repeat it at intervals. Chances are you'll wear him or her down, or your boss will notice the bad behavior and do something about it.

Within reasonable limits, let go of the need for control.

Your peace of mind—and your blood pressure—will suffer if you spend an excessive amount of time trying to control things you can't, such as your boss's or your coworkers' behavior. Instead, make sure you keep a healthy balance between work and play, that you have a life outside work. In your secretarial or administrative assistant job, you won't have the kind of control your boss has, and there's not much you can do about it. Don't let that fact give you an ulcer. Work is important, but it really shouldn't be regarded as a measure of your total worth.

FITTING INTO THE WORKPLACE CULTURE

Most of us want to belong to a group. It's the reason we have clubs and organizations and fraternities and sororities—and, I sometimes think, even armies. And yet fitting into a new group is one of the hardest things in the world.

To begin the process of fitting in at a workplace (and it is a process, not something that happens all at once), first think long and hard about the various kinds of workplaces out there (a review of chapter one will help refresh your memory). If you have a choice about where you work, make sure it's someplace you *want* to fit into.

After that, there are several things you can do, in terms of behavior and dress, for example, that will make fitting in easier.

Office Behavior

You should, of course, behave in the office according to the dictates of courtesy and common sense. Some good rules of thumb:

- Carry your load. Be on time for work, for staff meetings, and for other gatherings.
- Don't make too many personal phone calls (or any, if it's against company policy or if you're the only one doing it).
- Avoid interrupting your coworkers or your boss too often for minor matters. Avoid loud phone conversations or standing outside someone's cubicle chatting with a coworker.
- Strike a balance of formality—don't be either too familiar or too standoffish.

Office Attire

There are no real rules about dress. Conservative suits are appropriate in some situations; glitter eye shadow or ties that glow in the dark are appropriate in others. But some general rules apply:

- Look at what the other secretaries are wearing and take a cue from them. If there is no other secretary, look at the people in middle management. If you aspire to move up, look at what your boss is wearing and try to come as close as possible.

- Even as an executive secretary, don't exceed your budget just to impress people—you can be neat and stylish without spending a fortune.

- Whether your clothes are conservative or kooky (and there really is room for kooky clothes in some secretarial jobs—in a film company, for instance, or in a vet's office in which you might occasionally be called upon to corner someone's pet iguana that's scooted under your desk), be neat and clean, with shoes in good repair.

- Don't dress sloppily, but do dress comfortably. Don't wear clothes that are too tight. You'll feel miserable and awkward all day long.

MANAGING YOUR TIME

Next to good relationships with supervisors and coworkers, good time management is probably the most important aspect of any secretarial or administrative assistant job. (Actually, perhaps it's more important, because if you are a poor time manager, constantly harried and on edge, your relationships will suffer.)

To manage your time wisely, the first thing you need is a written agenda, a schedule that allows you to get all your work done during working hours, with a minimum of wasted time. It can be structured or quite informal, depending on your job demands and your temperament—anything from an hour-by-hour schedule to a simple priority list. For a complicated job, your daily agenda will be more complex, may change from day to day, and may include more frequent deadlines, so that you have to write daily tasks and deadlines on a calendar (if this is necessary, write the deadlines in red). If your tasks are more or less the same from day to day, a monthly agenda will work. (Do make a new agenda at least monthly to jog your memory about what's important and to ensure that you've taken any changes into account.)

Don't try to schedule your agenda too rigidly, down to the last minute, or you'll become frustrated. You may not be able to schedule in phone calls from Edna in the billing department, for example, because they seem to come at random, out of the blue. (Edna seems to have no agenda.) Nor can you schedule in the crises that Richard, your clerk-apprentice, always seems to be embroiled in. Neither can you schedule in socializing with your coworkers, although you know you'll do it (though not excessively, of course).

Create a To-Do List

Do a small amount of organization when you arrive at work each morning. For example, look at your agenda and do any small revisions needed. From tasks on your agenda, make a "to do" list for the day. If your boss likes to have an informal chat in the morning about the day's work, try to schedule it for first thing.

Set Priorities

Ask yourself which of your tasks for today or for this week is most important, and how much time it'll take. Be realistic. This is especially important if your job entails frequent deadlines. In some jobs you may have small, daily deadlines, and in others you may have huge, important deadlines spaced further apart—every two weeks or every month. For a heavily deadline-oriented job, in addition to your agenda you'll need a big calendar placed somewhere where you'll *see* it easily every day, to serve as a kind of task flowchart. Again, the important deadlines should be written clearly in red.

Make Use of Little Chunks of Time

Notice how time leaks away in droplets, and sometimes the day is over before you know it? Well, time can be *added to* in the same way. If you have five minutes before lunch and you just finished typing a report, there's no reason you can't start another, even if you won't finish it until after you get back. Or you can do just a small part of some pesky job you hate—file 5 invoices out of a stack of 50. You might make that quick call to Mike in accounting, if that's on your "to do" list (and if Mike's not much of a talker). If you seem to be perpetually on hold for Tiffany in the advertising department, take those moments to straighten things in your desk organizer that have been knocked askew. Do anything except sit there staring blankly at the clock. You'll be amazed at what you can accomplish. More important, it will improve your attitude by giving you a feeling of control over where the day goes.

PROMOTING YOURSELF

If, after you've been on the job a while, you decide to ask for a promotion or a raise, there are several things to consider.

First, be sure you really *want* the promotion.

Getting ahead, climbing up that ladder to success, bettering ourselves vocationally—we're all programmed to believe these are good things, and they are, usually. But the very first and most important question you must ask yourself, before you begin that dizzying ascent, is "Do I *want* to get ahead in this particular office, or are things just fine the way they are?"

This isn't as silly as it sounds. Legitimate reasons you might want to stay in your current position include:

- You job is rewarding and stable, and you like your boss and coworkers.
- Your family life or your avocation outside of work is important to you, and you don't want added job responsibilities that might sap your creative energy or your time with those you love.
- You don't yet have the skills you need for the next-level job. (If you lack the skills, however, you can begin work on acquiring them.)

To help you decide whether you really want to move to the next level in your company or organization, make a list of pros and cons for comparison. For example:

PROS	CONS
More creative work in new job	More comfort and confidence right where I am
Higher pay	Less time to spend with the kids in new job
Greater challenge and more responsibility	Less free time in new job for dog-walking, water skiing, gourmet cooking, rifle practice
Higher prestige	Higher stress level in new job

Spend time on this list—it's one of the most important ones you'll ever make and should contain as many items as you can think of. Examine yourself, your real interests, your likes and dislikes; try to think where you want to be five years from now.

Getting a Raise or Promotion

If you make up your mind you do want to get ahead, here are some suggestions:

- Research the job in question, and make sure you know that you have the skills to do it.
- Plan ahead. Continually upgrade your skills.
- Volunteer to take on additional projects.
- Do a little extra on the social front as well. Join your office's softball team (but *only* if you like softball) or volunteer to help plan a fundraiser or the company picnic.
- Network, formally and informally.
- Look at bulletin boards for posted jobs you might advance to. If you find a department you'd like to work in, try to get to know someone in it.
- Take an active interest in what the company or organization is doing.
- Read the trade journals and the company newsletter. Find out as much as you can about the product the company makes or the kinds of activities the organization sponsors.

When it comes time to ask for a raise or promotion, use moderation in your approach. Don't aggressively demand the job or raise, but don't go in with a "What a worm am I" attitude either. If you've researched the job you think you'd like to have, know you have the skills, and are excited about taking on the extra responsibility, your enthusiasm and confidence will show.

Don't be too disappointed or wail loudly if you don't get the raise or promotion. This might hurt your chances of getting it next time. Promotions and pay are often based not solely on who's most qualified, but on how long a person has been with the company or organization. Don't get impatient. If it's right, it'll happen.

FINDING A MENTOR

One of the best ways to get ahead in your job is to find a mentor, a wise counselor to help you. Sadly, in this day of cost-cutting layoffs, it may be more difficult to find a mentor than it once was, because many people who were happy to be mentors in the past are now afraid of losing their own jobs to younger (and lower-paid) employees. However, with some effort, you can find the right person to help you along your path.

A mentor advises you in the career you've chosen and (usually) in the ways of the organization for which you work. A good mentor empowers you and encourages you to use all your talents within your chosen career. A mentor can be older or younger than you; what's important is that he or she has been in the business longer.

Following is advice on finding a mentor even in this day of downsizing paranoia—advice that will work as well for administrative assistants as for executives.

First, you need not have just one mentor. Certainly you should seek a mentor (or several) within your place of employment, but as a November 1997 article in *Fortune* magazine suggests, you need not limit your search to your own company or organization. A mentor from outside will do just as well, as long as it's someone in the same field and someone you trust.

The article suggests you seek wise counsel from three kinds of mentors within your place of employment:

- a "higher up" (but not your boss, or you might be accused of simply currying favor) who can give you informal soundings on what your superiors think of your work
- a peer from another area of your place of employment, who can teach you about aspects of the company or organization you do not yet know
- a subordinate (if you're in a position of authority as, say, office manager), who can tell you what your "troops" think of your supervisory style

On the other hand, if you're not fortunate enough to have such an array of advisors, a mentor can simply be a friend who's had more experience than you in your chosen profession—someone you work with or someone you know from your other life. The person can be of the opposite or same gender, from your own ethnic group or from outside it. The important thing is that he or she be someone you trust and respect who's available to meet regularly for the purpose of discussing your career.

How do you find a mentor? The three best ways are:

- Join a professional organization. One of the very best is Professional Secretaries International, which has local chapters throughout the United States. (See Appendix A for the home office address.)
- "Court" an individual mentor in your place of employment or outside it. Invite that person for coffee or lunch. Be frank—say that you want to succeed in your job and therefore want to know as much about how to do so as possible. Most people like to talk about their work, and most people

like to give advice. If the first potential mentor doesn't work out, don't be discouraged. Look around for another prospect.

* Choose a friend who works in the same or a similar field. Ask that person to meet with you regularly, perhaps in a restaurant you both like, to discuss your job. Offer to buy, or invite the person to your house for a gourmet treat.

MOVING ON

Suppose you decide, after several years (or even months!), that your shiny new job isn't all you thought it would be. Or suppose it *is*, but now you've gained so much skill and knowledge that you've outgrown the company you work for. It's okay to change companies or organizations, as long as you don't do it too frequently or for the wrong reasons.

Kay May, executive secretary at American Express, says that at the beginning of her career, she quit her first job after six months. After finishing a nine-month course at Alexandria Vocational-Technical School in Virginia, she arrived in the Twin Cities in 1979 and got a job that she simply did not like. "I quit that job and went to Investors Diversified Services (IDS, later bought by American Express), and I've been there ever since."

Within American Express, Kay has changed titles several times, working first as a receptionist, then moving up to general secretary with the traditional duties of typing, filing, and answering phones, then again moving up to district secretary to Doug Lennick, executive vice president of the Private Client Group. She finally was promoted to executive secretary and now has many and varied responsibilities and perks—including taking daytrips on the corporate jet about 10 times a year to some of the 170 division office locations. She loves her job, but she would not have it if she hadn't had the courage to get out of a position that did not suit her.

Of course, you don't want to change jobs willy-nilly, or you'll soon find yourself unemployable. But there are legitimate reasons for moving on—for instance, the following:

* You've learned new skills or improved old ones to the point where your current job is no longer challenging.
* You like your job but don't find what your company or organization does very interesting.

- There's a subject you've always been fascinated by, and you'd like an administrative assistant position connected with it in some way (fashion design, police work, politics, law, medicine, or landscaping).
- You're moving to a new town.
- You dislike your job or the office atmosphere for any one of a variety of reasons (dull work, abusive boss, unethical business practices, or simply lack of anything meaningful in common with your coworkers).
- You're pretty sure the company you work for is downsizing, or you sense it's in financial trouble. Don't rely on gossip—make absolutely sure—but sometimes the signs are unmistakable. (In a job I had once, working as secretary to the president and part owner of a music and dance school, I put on my transcription headphones one morning and found that my first task was to type my boss's resume!)

If you decide you have sound, legitimate reasons for moving on, refer back to chapter five. Much of the advice on landing your first job will work as well for landing your second!

Sooner or later, you'll end up in a job you love, a satisfying and—who knows?—perhaps even exceptionally lucrative position that makes use of all your energy, training, and talent and fulfills many of your hopes and dreams.

THE INSIDE TRACK

Who:	Kay May
What:	Executive secretary to the executive vice president of American Express Financial Advisors
Where:	Minneapolis, Minnesota
How long:	Since 1981

Insider's Advice

Find a boss you have rapport with, then work on keeping the lines of communication open—rapport with your boss is the most important aspect of a job. Of course, it's important to remember who the boss is and to be flexible, but it's also important to have a boss who allows you to express yourself openly. I'm able to work fairly independently within certain boundaries. I open all mail and do first drafts of correspondence, and I do a lot of logistical stuff regarding my boss's travels and decide where he'll be going next. Our department does financial advising to individuals, and my boss has told all the advisors to go through me first rather than start with him. I take complaints and route them to the right place, passing on only those that are relevant to his work. I troubleshoot, giving him the opportunity to do what he was hired to do rather than getting bogged down in things that are irrelevant to his job.

Insider's Take on the Future

I'll stay where I am because I love my job, and I'm lucky to have a boss who trusts me to take all the responsibility I'm capable of. Many bosses seem to need to hang on to control so tightly that their secretaries don't get a chance to do what they're trained to do. I'm fortunate to have a boss who tells me the boundaries, then lets me go and trusts I'll do my job.

APPENDIX A

In addition to contact information for administrative assistant professional associations, this appendix lists national and regional accrediting agencies which you can contact to see if your chosen school is accredited. You'll also find a state-by-state listing of higher education agencies that provide information about financial aid.

PROFESSIONAL ASSOCIATIONS

This appendix contains a list of professional associations that can offer you relevant information related to enployment or training in the administrative assistant/secretary field.

ADMINISTRATIVE ASSISTANT/SECRETARY PROFESSIONAL ASSOCIATIONS

Here is a list of professional associations for administrative assistants and secretaries.

American Association of Medical Assistants
20 North Wacker Dr., Suite 1575
Chicago, IL 60606-2903
312-899-1500

National Association of Educational Office Professionals
P.O. Box 12619
1841 Eisenhower Court
Wichita, KS 67277-2619
316-942-4822

National Association of Executive Secretaries and
Administrative Assistants
900 S. Washington St., #G13
Falls Church, VA 22046
703-237-8616

National Association of Legal Secretaries (International)
2250 East 73rd St., Suite 550
Tulsa, OK 74136
918-493-3540

Professional Secretaries International
10502 NW Ambassador Dr.
Kansas City, MO 64195-0404
816-891-6600

NATIONAL ACCREDITING AGENCIES

Here is a list of national accrediting agencies for you to contact to see if your chosen school is accredited. You can request a list of schools that each agency accredits.

Accrediting Commission for Career Schools and Colleges
of Technology (ACCSCT)
Thomas A. Kube, Executive Director
2101 Wilson Blvd., Suite 302
Arlington, VA 22201
703-247-4212; FAX: 703-247-4533; e-mail: tkube@accsct.org

Accrediting Council for Independent Colleges and Schools (ACICS)
Stephen D. Parker, Executive Director
750 First St. NE, Suite 980
Washington, DC 20002-4241
 202-336-6780; FAX: 202-842-2593; e-mail: acics@digex.net

Distance Education and Training Council (DETC)
Michael P. Lambert, Executive Secretary
1601 Eighteenth St. NW
Washington, DC 20009-2529
 202-234-5100; FAX: 202-332-1386; e-mail: detc@detc.org

REGIONAL ACCREDITING AGENCIES

Middle States
Middle States Association of Colleges and Schools
Commission on Institutions of Higher Education
3624 Market St.
Philadelphia, PA 19104-2680
215-662-5606; FAX: 215-662-5950; e-mail: jamorse@msache.org

New England States
Charles M. Cook, Director
New England Association of Schools and Colleges
Commission on Institutions of Higher Education (NEASC-CIHE)
209 Burlington Rd.
Bedford, MA 07130-1433
617-271-0022; FAX: 617-271-0950; e-mail: ccook@neasc.org

Richard E. Mandeville, Director
New England Association of Schools and Colleges
Commission on Vocational, Technical and Career Institution (NEASC-CTCI)
209 Burlington Rd.
Bedford, MA 01730-1433
617-271-0022: FAX: 617-271-0950; e-mail: rmandeville@neasc.org

North Central States

Steve Crow, Executive Director
North Central Association of Colleges and Schools
Commission on Institutions of Higher Education (NCA)
30 North LaSalle, Suite 2400
Chicago, IL 60602-2504
312-263-0456; FAX: 312-263-7462; e-mail: crow@ncacihe.org

Northwest States

Sandra Elman, Executive Director
Northwest Association of Schools and Colleges
Commission on Colleges
11130 NE 33rd Pl., Suite 120
Bellevue, WA 98004
206-827-2005; FAX: 206-827-3395; e-mail: selman@u.washington.edu

Southern States

James T. Rogers, Executive Director
Southern Association of Colleges and Schools
Commission on Colleges (SACS)
1866 Southern Ln.
Decatur, GA 30033-4097
404-679-4500; 800-248-7701; FAX: 404-679-4558; e-mail: jrogers@sacscoc.org

Western States

David B. Wolf, Executive Director
Western Association of Schools and Colleges
Accrediting Commission for Community and Junior Colleges (WASC-Jr.)
3402 Mendocino Ave.
Santa Rosa, CA 95403-2244
707-569-9177; FAX: 707-569-9179; e-mail: ACCJC@aol.com

Ralph A. Wolff, Executive Director

Western Association of Schools and Colleges

Accrediting Commission for Senior Colleges and Universities (WASC-Sr.)

c/o Mills College, Box 9990

Oakland, CA 94613-0990

510-632-5000; FAX: 510-632-8361; e-mail: rwolff@wasc.mills.educ

FINANCIAL AID FROM STATE HIGHER EDUCATION AGENCIES

You can request information about financial aid from each of the following state higher education agencies and governing boards.

ALABAMA

Alabama Commission on Higher Education

Suite 205

3465 Norman Bridge Rd.

Montgomery 36105-2310

334-281-1998; http://www.alsde.edu/

State Department of Education

Gordon Persons Office Building

50 North Ripley St.

Montgomery 36130-3901

205-242-8082

ALASKA

Alaska Commission on Postsecondary Education

3030 Vintage Boulevard

Juneau 99801-7109

907-465-2962; http://sygov.swadm.alaska.edu/BOR/

State Department of Education

Goldbelt Place

801 West 10th St., Suite 200

Juneau 99801-1894

907-465-8715; http://www.educ.state.ak.us

ARIZONA

Arizona Commission for Postsecondary Education
2020 North Central Ave., Suite 275
Phoenix 85004-4503
602- 229-2531; http://www.abor.asu.edu

State Department of Education
1535 West Jefferson
Phoenix 85007
602-542-2147; http://www.ade.state.az.us/

ARKANSAS

Arkansas Department of Higher Education
114 East Capitol
Little Rock 72201-3818
501-324-9300

Arkansas Department of Education
4 State Capitol Mall, Room 304A
Little Rock 72201-1071
501-682-4474; http://arkedu.k12.ar.us//

CALIFORNIA

California Student Aid Commission
P.O. Box 510845
Sacramento 94245-0845
916-445-0880; http://www.ucop.edu/ucophome/system/regents.html

1515 South St., North Bldg.
Suite 500, P.O. Box 510845
Sacramento 94245-0621
916-322-2294

California Department of Education
721 Capitol Mall
Sacramento 95814
916-657-2451; http://goldmine.cde.ca.gov

COLORADO

Colorado Commission on Higher Education
Colorado Heritage Center
1300 Broadway, 2nd Fl.
Denver 80203
303-866-2723; http://www.state.co.us/edu_dir/state_hredu_dept.html

State Department of Education
201 E. Colfax Ave.
Denver 80203-1705
303-866-6779; http://www.cde.state.co.us

CONNECTICUT

Connecticut Department of Higher Education
61 Woodland St.
Hartford 06105-2391
203-566-3910; http://www.lib.uconn.edu/ConnState/HigherEd/dhe.htm

Connecticut Department of Education
165 Capitol Ave., P.O. Box 2219
Hartford 06106-1630
http://www.aces.k12.ct.us/csde

DELAWARE

Delaware Higher Education Commission
Carvel State Office Bldg., 4th Fl.
820 North French St.
Wilmington 19801
302-577-3240; http://www.state.de.us/high-ed/commiss/webpage.htm

State Department of Public Instruction
Townsend Building #279
Federal and Lockerman Sts.
P.O. Box 1402
Dover 19903-1402
302-739-4583; http://www.dpi.state.de.us/dpi/dpi/dpi.html

DISTRICT OF COLUMBIA
Department of Human Services
Office of Postsecondary Education, Research, and Assistance
2100 Martin Luther King Jr. Ave. SE, Suite 401
Washington 20020
202-727-3685

District of Columbia Public Schools
Division of Student Services
4501 Lee St. NE
Washington 20019
202-724-4934; http://www.k12.dc.us/DCPSHP.html

FLORIDA
Florida Department of Education
Office of Student Financial Assistance
1344 Florida Education Ctr.
325 West Gaines St.
Tallahassee 32399-0400
904-487-0649; http://www.nwrdc.fsu.edu/bor

GEORGIA
Georgia Student Finance Authority
State Loans and Grants Division
Suite 245, 2082 E. Exchange Pl.
Tucker 30084
404-414-3000; http://www.peachnet.edu/BORWEB

State Department of Education
2054 Twin Towers E., 205 Butler St.
Atlanta 30334-5040
404-656-5812; http://www.doe.state.ga.us

HAWAII
Hawaii State Postsecondary Education Commission
2444 Dole St., Rm. 202
Honolulu 96822-2394
808-956-8213; http://www.hern.hawaii.edu/hern

Hawaii Department of Education
2530 10th Ave., Rm. A12
Honolulu 96816
808-733-9103; http://www.doe.hawaii.edu

IDAHO
Idaho Board of Education
P.O. Box 83720
Boise 83720-0037
208-334-2270

State Department of Education
650 West State St.
Boise 83720
208-334-2113; http://www.sde.state.id.us/

ILLINOIS
Illinois Student Assistance Commission
1755 Lake Cook Rd.
Deerfield 60015-5209
708-948-8500

INDIANA
State Student Assistance Commission of Indiana
Suite 500, 150 W. Market St.
Indianapolis 46204-2811
317-232-2350; http://www.ai.org/ssaci

Indiana Department of Education
Rm. 229, State House
Center for Schools Improvement and Performance
Indianapolis 46204-2798
317-232-2305; http://ideanet.doe.state.in.us:80

IOWA

Iowa College Student Aid Commission
914 Grand Ave., Suite 201
Des Moines 50309-2824
800-383-4222; http://www.state.ia.us/government/icsac/index.htm

Iowa Department of Education
http://www.state.ia.us/educate

KANSAS

Kansas Board of Regents
700 S.W. Harrison, Suite 1410
Topeka 66603-3760
913-296-3517

State Department of Education
Kansas State Education Bldg.
120 E. Tenth St.
Topeka 66612-1103
913-296-4876

KENTUCKY

Kentucky Higher Education Assistance Authority
Suite 102, 1050 U.S. 127 S.
Frankfort 40601-4323
800-928-8926

State Department of Education
500 Mero St.
1919 Capital Plaza Tower
Frankfort 40601
502-564-3421; http://www.kde.state.ky.us

LOUISIANA

Louisiana Student Financial Assistance Commission
Office of Student Financial Assistance
P.O. Box 91202

Baton Rouge 70821-9202
800-259-5626

State Department of Education
P.O. Box 94064
626 North 4th St., 12th Fl.
Baton Rouge 70804-9064
504-342-2098; http://www.doe.state.la.us

MAINE

Finance Authority of Maine
P.O. Box 949
Augusta 04333-0949
207-287-3263; http://www.maine.edu

Maine Department of Education
23 State House Sta.
Augusta 04333-0023
207-287-5800; TDD/TTY 207-287-2550; FAX: 207-287-5900;
http://www.state.me.us/education/homepage.htm

MARYLAND

Maryland Higher Education Commission
Jeffrey Building, 16 Francis St.
Annapolis 21401-1781
410-974-2971; http://www.ubalt.edu/www/mhec

Maryland State Department of Education
200 West Baltimore St.
Baltimore 21201-2595
410-767-0480; http://www.maryland.umd.edu/mde.html

MASSACHUSETTS

Massachusetts Board of Higher Education
330 Stuart St.
Boston 02116
617-727-9420

State Department of Education
350 Main St.
Malden 02148-5023
617-388-3300; http://www.doe.mass.edu/

Massachusetts Higher Education Information Center
666 Boylston St.
Boston 02116
617-536-0200 x4719; http://www.heic.org

MICHIGAN
Michigan Higher Education Assistance Authority
Office of Scholarships and Grants
P.O. Box 30462
Lansing 48909-7962
517-373-3394

Michigan Department of Education
608 W. Allegan St., Hannah Building
Lansing 48909
517-373-3324; http://web.mde.state.mi.us

MINNESOTA
Minnesota Higher Education Services Office
Suite 400, Capitol Square Bldg.
550 Cedar St.
St. Paul 55101-2292
800-657-3866; gopher://gopher.hecb.state.mn.us/

Department of Children, Families, and Learning
712 Capitol Sq. Bldg.
550 Cedar St.
St. Paul 55101
612-296-6104; gopher://gopher.educ.state.mn.us/HOME.HTM

MISSISSIPPI

Mississippi Postsecondary Education
Financial Assistance Board
3825 Ridgewood Rd.
Jackson 39211-6453
601-982-6663

State Department of Education
P.O. Box 771
Jackson 39205-0771
601-359-3768; http://mdek12.state.ms.us/

MISSOURI

Missouri Coordinating Board for Higher Education
3515 Amazonas Dr.
Jefferson City 65109-5717
314-751-2361; gopher://dp.mocbhe.gov

Missouri State Department of Elementary and Secondary Education
P.O. Box 480
205 Jefferson St., Sixth Fl.
Jefferson City 65102-0480
314-751-2931; http://services.dese.state.mo.us

MONTANA

Montana University System
2500 Broadway
Helena 59620-3103
406-444-6570; http://www.montana.edu/~aircj/manual/bor

State Office of Public Instruction
State Capitol, Rm. 106
Helena 59620
406-444-4422; http://161.7.114.15/OPI/opi.html

NEBRASKA

Coordinating Commission for Postsecondary Education
P.O. Box 95005
Lincoln 68509-5005
402-471-2847

Nebraska Department of Education
P.O. Box 94987
301 Centennial Mall S.
Lincoln 68509-4987
402-471-2784; http://www.nde.state.ne.us/

NEVADA

Nevada Department of Education
400 West King St., Capitol Complex
Carson City 89710
702-687-5915; http://nsn.scs.unr.edu/nvdoe

NEW HAMPSHIRE

New Hampshire Postsecondary Education Commission
2 Industrial Park Dr.
Concord 03301-8512
603-271-2555

State Department of Education
State Office Park South
101 Pleasant St.
Concord 03301
603-271-2632; http://www.state.nh.us/doe/education.html

NEW JERSEY

State of New Jersey
Office of Student Financial Assistance
4 Quakerbridge Plaza, CN 540
Trenton 08625
800-792-8670; http://ww.state.nj.us/highereducation/

State Department of Education
225 West State St.
Trenton 08625-0500
609-984-6409; http://www.state.nj.us/education

NEW MEXICO

New Mexico Commission on Higher Education
1068 Cerrillos Rd.
Santa Fe 87501-4925
505-827-7383; http://www.nmche.org/index.html

State Department of Education
Education Building
300 Don Gaspar
Santa Fe 87501-2786
505-827-6648; http://sde.state.nm.us/

NEW YORK

New York State Higher Education Services Corporation
One Commerce Plaza
Albany 12255
518-474-5642; http://hesc.state.ny.us

State Education Department
111 Education Bldg., Washington Ave.
Albany 12234
518-474-5705; http://www.nysed.gov/

NORTH CAROLINA

North Carolina State Education Assistance Authority
P.O. Box 2688
Chapel Hill 27515-2688
919-821-4771

State Department of Public Instruction
Education Building, Division of Teacher Education
116 West Edenton St.
Raleigh 27603-1712
919-733-0701; http://www.dpi.state.nc.us/

NORTH DAKOTA

North Dakota University System
North Dakota Student Financial Assistance Program
600 E. Boulevard Ave.
Bismarck 58505-0230
701-224-4114

State Department of Public Instruction
State Capitol Bldg., 11th Fl.
600 E. Boulevard Ave.
Bismarck 58505-0164
701-224-2271; http://www.sendit.nodak.edu/dpi

OHIO

Ohio Student Aid Commission
P.O. Box 182452
309 South Fourth St.
Columbus 43218-2452
800-837-6752; http://www.bor.ohio.gov

State Department of Education
65 South Front St., Rm. 1005
Columbus 43266-0308
614-466-2761; http://www.ode.ohio.gov

OKLAHOMA

Oklahoma State Regents for Higher Education
http://www.osrhe.edu

Oklahoma Guaranteed Student Loan Program
P.O. Box 3000
Oklahoma City 73101-3000
405-858-4300; 800-247-0420; http://www.ogslp.org

State Department of Education
Oliver Hodge Memorial Education Bldg.
2500 North Lincoln Blvd.
Oklahoma City 73105-4599
405-521-4122; gopher://gopher.osrhe.edu

OREGON
Oregon State Scholarship Commission
Suite 100, 1500 Valley River Dr.
Eugene 97401-2130
503-687-7400; http://www.teleport.com/~ossc/home.htm

Oregon State System of Higher Education
700 Pringle Parkway, S.E.
Salem 97310-0290
503-378-5585; http://www.osshe.edu

Oregon Department of Education
255 Capitol St. NE
Salem 97310-0203
http://www.ode.state.or.us

PENNSYLVANIA
Pennsylvania Higher Education Assistance Agency
1200 North Seventh St.
Harrisburg 17102-1444
800-692-7435; http://sshe2.sshechan.edu/sshe.html

RHODE ISLAND
Rhode Island Board of Governors for Higher Education
http://www.ids.net/ribog/riohe.htm

Rhode Island Office of Higher Education
301 Promenade St.
Providence 02908-5720
401-277-6560; FAX: 401-277-6111;
RIBOG@uriacc.uri.edu; http://www.ids.net/ribog/index.htm

Rhode Island Higher Education Assistance Authority
560 Jefferson Blvd.
Warwick 02886
800-922-9855

State Department of Education
22 Hayes St.
Providence 02908
401-277-3126; http://www.ri.net/RIDE

SOUTH CAROLINA

South Carolina Higher Education Tuition Grants Commission
1310 Lady St., Suite 811
P.O. Box 12159
Columbia 29201
803-734-1200; http://che400.state.sc.us

State Department of Education
803-a Rutledge Bldg.
1429 Senate St.
Columbia 29201
803-734-8364; http://www.state.sc.us/sde

SOUTH DAKOTA

Department of Education and Cultural Affairs
Office of the Secretary
700 Governors Dr.
Pierre 57501-2291
605-773-3134; http://www.state.sd.us/state/executive/deca/deca.html

South Dakota Board of Regents
http://www.ris.sdbor.edu

TENNESSEE

Tennessee Higher Education Commission
404 James Robertson Pkwy., Suite 1900
Nashville 37243-0820
615-741-3605; http://www.TBR.state.tn.us

State Department of Education
100 Cordell Hull Bldg.
Nashville 37219-5335
615-741-1346; 800-342-1663 (TN residents only);
http://www.state.tn.us/other/sde/homepage.htm

TEXAS

Texas Higher Education Coordinating Board
P.O. Box 12788, Capitol Station
Austin 78711
800-242-3062; http://www.texas.gov/agency/781.html

UTAH

Utah State Board of Regents
Utah System of Higher Education
355 West North Temple
#3 Triad Center, Suite 550
Salt Lake City 84180-1205
801-321-7205; http://www.gv.ex.state.ut.us/highered.htm

Utah State Office of Education
250 East 500 S.
Salt Lake City 84111
801-538-7779; http://www.usoe.k12.ut.us

VERMONT

Vermont Student Assistance Corporation
Champlain Mill
P.O. Box 2000
Winooski 05404-2601
800-642-3177; http://www.vsac.org

Vermont Department of Education
120 State St.
Montpelier 05620-2501
802-828-3147; FAX: 802-828-3140; http://www.state.vt.us/educ

VIRGINIA

State Council of Higher Education for Virginia
James Monroe Bldg., 101 N. 14th St.
Richmond 23219
804-225-2137; http://www.schev.edu

State Department of Education
P.O. Box 2120
Richmond 23218-2120
800-292-3820; http://pen1.pen.k12.va.us/Anthology/VDOE

WASHINGTON

Washington State Higher Education Coordinating Board
P.O. Box 43430, 917 Lakeridge Way, SW
Olympia 98504-3430
206-753-7850

State Department of Public Instruction
Old Capitol Bldg., P.O. Box FG 11
Olympia 98504-3211
206-753-2858; http://www.ospi.wednet.edu/

WEST VIRGINIA

State Department of Education
1900 Washington St., Bldg. B, Rm. 358
Charleston 25305
304-588-2691

State College and University Systems of West Virginia Central Office
1018 Kanawha Blvd. E., Suite 700
Charleston 25301-2827
304-558-4016; http://www.scusco.wvnet.edu

WISCONSIN

Higher Educational Aids Board
P.O. Box 7885
Madison 53707-7885
608-267-2206; http://www.uwsa.edu/

State Department of Public Instruction
125 South Wester St.
P.O. Box 7841
Madison 53707-7814
608-266-2364; http://www.state.wi.us/agencies/dpi

WYOMING

Wyoming State Department of Education
Hathaway Bldg., 2300 Capitol Ave., 2nd Fl.
Cheyenne 82002-0050
307-777-6265; http://www.k12.wy.us/wdehome.html

Wyoming Community College Commission
2020 Carey Ave., 8th Fl.
Cheyenne 82002
307-777-7763

PUERTO RICO

Council on Higher Education
Box 23305, UPR Station
Rio Piedras 00931
809-758-3350

Department of Education
P.O. Box 759
Hato Rey 00919
809-753-2200

U.S. DEPARTMENT OF EDUCATION

SSIG Program
Office of Postsecondary Education
Student Financial Assistance Programs, Pell and State Grant Section
U.S. Department of Education
ROB #3, Rm. 3045, 600 Independence Ave. SW
Washington, DC 20202-5447
202-708-4607

Byrd Program
Division of Higher Education Incentive Programs
Higher Education Programs
Office of Postsecondary Education
U.S. Department of Education
1280 Maryland Ave. SW, Suite C80
Washington, DC 20024

APPENDIX B

After you've been through this entire book and have a good idea of what steps you need to take to accomplish your goals, look through this appendix for titles that will give you more specific advice on areas you need help in.

ADDITIONAL RESOURCES

For additional information on the topics discussed in this book, refer to the following reading lists, which are organized by subject, and the list of job-related Web sites that follows.

Colleges

Peterson's Guide to Two-Year Colleges 1998: The Only Guide to More than 1,500 Community and Junior Colleges. Princeton, NJ: Peterson's . 1997.

The College Board, *The College Handbook 1998.* 35th Ed. New York: College Entrance Exam Board. 1997.

The Princeton Review, *The Complete Book of Colleges 1998.* New York: Random House, The Princeton Review. 1997.

Cover Letters

Beatty, Richard H., *The Perfect Cover Letter.* 2nd Ed. New York: John Wiley & Sons. 1997.

Besson, Taunee, *The Wall Street Journal National Business Employment Weekly: Cover Letters*. 2nd Ed. New York: John Wiley & Sons. 1996.

Marler, Patty and Jan Bailey Mattia, *Cover Letters Made Easy*. Lincolnwood, IL: VGM Career Horizons. 1996.

Yate, Martin, *Cover Letters That Knock 'em Dead*. Holbrook, MA: Adams Publishing. 1995.

Financial Aid

Chany, Kalman A. and Geoff Martz, *Student Advantage Guide to Paying for College 1997 Edition*. New York: Random House, The Princeton Review. 1997.

College School Service, *College Costs & Financial Aid Handbook*. 18th Ed. New York: The College Entrance Examination Board. 1998.

Davis, Kristen, *Financing College: How to Use Savings, Financial Aid, Scholarships, and Loans to Afford the School of Your Choice*. Washington, DC: Random House, Kiplinger. 1996.

See also Chapter Four and the Scholarships section, below.

Internships

Hamadeh, Samer and Mark Oldham, *America's Top Internships 1997*. 3rd Ed. New York: Random House, The Princeton Review. 1996.

Srinivasan, Kalpana and *The Yale Daily News*, *The Yale Daily News Guide to Internships 1998 Edition*. New York: Simon & Schuster. 1997.

Interviews

Bloch, Deborah P., Ph.D., *How to Have A Winning Interview*. Lincolnwood, IL: VGM Career Horizons. 1996.

Fry, Ron, *101 Great Answers to the Toughest Interview Questions*. 3rd Ed. Franklin Lakes, NJ: Book-Mart Press. 1996.

Kennedy, Joyce Lain, *Job Interviews for Dummies*. Foster City, CA: IDG Books. 1996.

General Job Hunting

Bureau of Labor Statistics, *Dictionary of Occupational Titles*. 4th Ed. Vol. 1, 2. Bureau of Labor Statistics. 1991.

Bureau of Labor Statistics, *Occupational Outlook Handbook 1996–1997*.

Cubbage, Sue A. and Marcia P. Williams, *The 1996 National Job Hotline Directory*. New York: McGraw-Hill. 1996.

General Office References

Merriam-Webster's Secretarial Handbook. Springfield, MA: Merriam-Webster, 1993.

Complete Office Handbook: The Definitive Reference for Today's Electronic Office. New York: Random House, 1997.

The above two books will give you a good idea of what administrative assistant work entails.

Networking

National Business Employment Weekly, *Networking: Insider's Strategies for Tapping the Hidden Market Where Most Jobs are Found*. New York: John Wiley & Sons, 1994.

Office Politics

Bell, Arthur and Dayle M. Smith, *Winning With Difficult People*. New York: Barron's Educational Series, 1991.

Bramson, Robert M., Ph.D., *Coping With Difficult People*. New York: Anchor Press, 1981.

Felder, Leonard, *Does Someone at Work Treat You Badly?* New York: Berkely Books, 1993.

Tarbell, Shirley, *Office Basics Made Easy*. New York, LearningExpress, 1997.

Resumes

Adams Resume Almanac & Disc. Holbrook, MA: Adams Media Corporation. 1996.

Haft, Timothy D., *Trashproof Resumes: Your Guide to Cracking the Job Market*. Princeton, NJ: Princeton Review, 1995.

The Guide to Basic Resume Writing. Chicago: VGM Career Horizons, NTC Publishing Group, 1991.

Scholarship Guides

Cassidy, Daniel J., *The Scholarship Book: The Complete Guide to Private-Sector Scholarships, Grants, and Loans for Undergraduates*. Englewood Cliffs, NJ: Prentice Hall. 1996.

Ragins, Marianne, *Winning Scholarships for College: An Insider's Guide.* New York: Henry Holt & Co. 1994.

Scholarships, Grants & Prizes: Guide to College Financial Aid From Private Sources. Princeton, NJ: Peterson's. 1998.

Schwartz, John, *College Scholarships and Financial Aid.* New York: Simon & Schuster, Macmillan. 1995.

Scholarships 1998 . New York: Simon & Schuster, Kaplan. 1997.

Studying

How to Study (A part of the *Basics Made Easy* series). New York: LearningExpress. 1997.

Read Better, Remember More (A part of the *Basics Made Easy* series). New York: LearningExpress. 1997.

Test Help

ACT: Powerful Strategies to Help You Score Higher. 1998 Edition. Kaplan. New York: Simon & Schuster. 1997.

Katyman, John and Adam Robinson, *Cracking the SAT & PSAT 1998 Edition.* New York: Random House, The Princeton Review. 1997.

Schroeder, Betty L. and Alan D. Kardoff, *Management (Certified Professional Secretary Examination Review).* New York: Prentice Hall, 1995.

The above is one in a series of CPS Exam Reviews; others include *Finance and Business Law, Office Systems and Administration, Accounting,* and *Behavioral Science in Business* (go to the Web site http://www.amazon.com for a complete list of titles under subject heading Certified Professional Secretary).

Helpful Job Search Web Sites

If you have access to the Internet, try checking out these helpful job search Web sites to find job openings, get career advice, look up salary information, read company profiles, and even post your resume at select sites.

Web Address and Name	Job Postings	Entry-level Jobs	Company Profiles	Salary Survey	Career Advice
http://www.careermosaic.com **Career Mosaic**	X	X	X		X
http://www.espan.com **e.span**	X		X		X
http://iccweb.com/employ.html **Internet Career Connection**	X	X			X
http://www.hoovers.com **Hoover's Online**			X		
http://www.intellimatch.com **Intellimatch**	X	X			
http://www.jobbankusa.com **Job Bank USA**	X	X			X
http://www.monster.com **The Monster Board**	X	X	X		X
http://www.occ.com **Online Career Center**	X	X			X
http://jobsource.com **JobSource**					X
http://www.zdnet.com/zdimag/salaryzone/ **Salary Zone**				X	X
http://www.careersite.com/ **Career Site**	X	X	X		
http://www.collegeview.com **College View**				X	X
http://www.jobsfed.com **Federal Jobs**	X	X			

APRIL 8, 1998